SLAYING THE THREE DRAGONS

Overcoming *Doubt*, *Worry*, and *Fear*

SLAYING THE THREE DRAGONS

Overcoming *Doubt*, *Worry*, and *Fear*

ANTHONY STRANO

STERLING ETHOS
An imprint of Sterling Publishing Co., Inc.

New York / London
www.sterlingpublishing.com

Library of Congress Cataloging-in-Publication Data

Strano, Anthony, 1951–
  Slaying the three dragons : overcoming doubt, worry, and fear / Anthony Strano.
    p. cm.
  Includes index.
  ISBN 978-1-4027-6640-4 (hardcover and CD : alk. paper) 1. Meditation–Brahmakumari. I. Title.
  BL1274.255.S77 2010
  294.5'435–dc22

2009032124

10 9 8 7 6 5 4 3

Published by Sterling Publishing Co., Inc.
387 Park Avenue South, New York, NY 10016
© 2010 by Brahma Kumaris Information Services Ltd.
Distributed in Canada by Sterling Publishing
^c/o Canadian Manda Group, 165 Dufferin Street
Toronto, Ontario, Canada M6K 3H6
Distributed in the United Kingdom by GMC Distribution Services
Castle Place, 166 High Street, Lewes, East Sussex, England BN7 1XU
Distributed in Australia by Capricorn Link (Australia) Pty. Ltd.
P.O. Box 704, Windsor, NSW 2756, Australia

Manufactured in China

Sterling ISBN 978-1-4027-6640-4

For information about custom editions, special sales, premium and corporate purchases, please contact Sterling Special Sales Department at 800-805-5489 or specialsales@sterlingpublishing.com.

∞ Contents ∞

∞ 1 ∞

Slaying the Three Dragons

IN A WORLD OF CONSTANT DEMANDS, where everything appears to happen at lightning speed, people want to learn the technique of freeing themselves from the variety of tensions they face, find an inner calm to bring about balance in their lives, and sustain a positive frame of mind. Some of the greatest challenges of contemporary life lie in everyday chaos, pervasive monsters that lurk in the back of our minds: the three great dragons of worry, doubt, and fear. Although we may combat them with pills or exercises, affirmations or quick-fix cures, many people are now accepting that we must look within ourselves before lashing out at the stresses that menace us. Many people agree that meditation is the best method of finding the inner peace that can give us strength in times of trial.

However, in the West, many people who wish to learn how to meditate do so only because they want to relax. In the East, meditation is an ancient tradition that involves far more than just relaxing and being positive: it is also a way to enlighten the mind. An enlightened mind is one filled with peace, clarity, and kindness. Clarity enables the individual to make decisions, which are benevolent and accurate for the self and others; kindness protects the self and others from the harmful effects of the mind's negative desires. The aim of meditation is to use the values of wisdom, peace, and kindness to enable the individual to control the mind, to keep it in order.

However, even in ancient times, the mind was understood to be extremely difficult to control. It was said to be like the wind: you could never catch it or hold it—it went where it wished, and no human being could become its master. In other instances, it was said that the mind was like an elephant: extremely powerful, but equally gentle and patient, able to do a lot of work for its master. However, when an elephant turns rogue, its gentleness and patience completely disappear and it destroys and damages everything in its path. When the mind is under stress, it resembles a rogue elephant: it has no control and cannot be controlled.

Taming the mind is regarded as a great art requiring time, attention, practice—and, above all, a sincerity of heart where individuals truly want to change their way of thinking. To relax, to be positive, to be peaceful and kind all require a change in our thought patterns, and this can only happen when we look deeply within. However hard they try, other people cannot change us; we must have personal realization and the desire to make changes through our own effort. Permanent and positive change cannot be imposed from the outside; it is something that we choose.

Meditation is the discovery of that point of silence within, like a compass needle that guides us in the right direction at the right time. To become silent, to be still in the ocean of hectic, noisy action, is a choice that many people are now making. When this is achieved, this stillness acts on the mind like oxygen, giving the breath to both understand and enrich life. Of course, action is a necessity, an expression of ourselves through time, relationships, and the roles we play. However, if we do not sometimes stop and take a breath of silence, then the mind begins to suffocate, thoughts speed like bullet trains, and the brain feels as if it is in a pressure cooker. Emotions erupt and react like volcanoes, the eyes become dizzy with mountains of information, and the head feels like a roller coaster. This is stress. The mind needs to come up for air; to leave the jungle of pressures, deadlines, and speed; and to slow down and find the point of silence within.

Meditation is the method to find that point which recharges the mind with peace, clarity, and balance.

We can define meditation as the eight "Rs".

1. Returning

Meditation is the technique of returning to the original qualities of the self: namely peace, purity, love, bliss, and wisdom. We can only do that by taking our thoughts inwards.

> *I begin to find my original strength by collecting the energy of my mind. With my concentrated thought, I focus on meeting my real self.*

2. Relaxing

In meditation, the mind disconnects itself from the thoughts of anything external and connects with the inner self. In this way, it is able to receive the positive current of the original strength of the self: a peaceful source of energy. However, at first it can be difficult to disconnect the many plugs of our everyday life: the plugs of attachment, speed, worry, being busy, and so forth. It does take some effort.

> *As I connect to the "point source" of energy of the self, which is located in the center of the forehead, I start to relax, to remove the many tensions and demands of the outside world from the mind.*

3. Remembering

As the mind relaxes and gently concentrates on the "point source" of peace energy, individuals begin to remember their spiritual identities. The reason why people are so disorientated in their lives and why they often find life boring, tedious, or empty is because they have forgotten who they truly are.

In silence, going inward, I begin to remember what I have forgotten: I am a spiritual being, a point source of positive energy. My spirit is my reality!

4. Releasing

As we remember the forgotten reality of the self as a spiritual being and begin to experience our inner source of peace, we are released from the negativity of our mind, wasteful thinking, and thoughts filled with doubt, fear, and worry—the three great dragons that dominate our mind.

As I begin to rule my own mind, I free myself from the worry that cripples my confidence, from the fear that hijacks my courage, and the doubt that ridicules every attempt I make to bring hope back into my life.

5. Relearning

As we become free, we begin to respect ourselves and relearn what it means to value our self, our life, and our existence in this great play of life. Forgotten truths appear, and a new education of the self begins.

I am able to understand eternity and spirituality, and feelings of my true humanity emerge.

6. Rediscovering

As we relearn, we rediscover our spiritual values and resources and, realizing that they were always there, we resolve to use these silent intrinsic truths, which are the foundation of a better quality of life.

> *I am a positive, purposeful being who has something unique to offer to life.*

7. Restoring

As we begin to use these spiritual truths, our original strengths and qualities are restored. There is a transition in consciousness that enables confidence and self-esteem to become a natural way of being.

> *I value myself as a being of peace and love and know that I have within me all the qualities I need to overcome all the challenges of life.*

8. Recharging

The leap of consciousness that occurs when we connect with our inner spiritual self is a powerful way of recharging the energies of the human mind. It is filled with a deep tranquility that first flows into our thoughts and is then reflected in our words and actions. A world of new vision opens where there is self-mastery and acceptance of life as it is.

> *I have the inner strength to let go of judgments, dissatisfaction, and impatience and to replace negative energies with a more positive outlook.*

∽ 2 ∽

Quality Change

QUALITY CHANGE IS THE CAPACITY TO TRANSFORM "negative" situations or circumstances into something beneficial for one's self and others. "Quality transformers" are people who can turn walls of resistance into bridges of understanding and keep crossing them, who can change any obstacle into a steppingstone of success and can reverse the niggling, paralyzing dragon of doubt into radiant self-confidence, dissolving the thought "impossible" from the mind.

Such people work with the undercurrents of life that determine the external reality of human interaction, namely their attitudes, thoughts, and feelings. If these are permeated with resentment, anger, and selfishness, then, despite a façade of politeness or cooperation, relationships will be subject to damage and deterioration. On the other hand, when the undercurrent is one of trust and sincerity, then the quality of life is enhanced. The fundamental source of quality is the existence of a positive undercurrent. It is not a matter of words, actions, or role, but rather the foundation of these, manifested in thoughts and the activity of the mind.

Meditation enables the mind to tune in to that undercurrent of thoughts, feelings, and attitudes, which is the invisible creator of our human reality. The nourishing power of silence, attained through meditation and spiritual knowledge, gives us the means to create quality change. Such change enhances our self-confidence and the capacity to creatively and positively relate to life as it is.

Silence gives us the energy necessary to effect change, and self-knowledge gives us the perception and insight to realize the opportunity for change that everyone and every situation offers.

How do we qualitatively transform ourselves? Is it something we plan and consciously do? Does it just happen by itself? Or is it a state of awareness that naturally recognizes opportunities for quality change?

The easiest way to understand quality change came to me one day when I needed to put fresh, smelly manure around the roses in my garden. After a few hours of this work, I realized that those beautiful flowers, although nourished by the manure, did not take on any of its odor or color. They were truly like kings of the garden, in their pink, gold, red, and white robes, filling the air with such a fragrance that people who came to the garden did not even notice the manure. The roots of the roses were able to transform the manure to such an extent that the best was taken without any negative side effects. This was my first experience of quality change.

The human world is like a garden. We are like a variety of flowers surrounded by lots of manure: that is, negativity in all its forms, such as ego, fear, anger, attachment, mistrust, and so on. People who are "quality transformers" can accept all these negative things and use them for their personal growth without the negativity penetrating them; they do not get spoiled, or even touched, by it. With understanding and the natural, loving detachment that comes from silence, they realize that the negative person, or situation, in front of them is the Universe's way of giving them an opportunity to create a tiny, silent miracle in their lives. Quality transformers become the spiritual roses in the Garden of Humanity: they display all their beauty and provide inspiration for all those who see them.

"Quality transformers" can also be compared to the oyster: when a tiny foreign particle invades its home, it secretes a liquid that combines with the particle to eventually create a pearl. The pearl can live in the oyster's home for the rest of the oyster's natural life without causing any disturbance.

In the same way, rather than react negatively to people and events, we can include them and mold with them. Through acceptance, our consciousness jumps to another level of perception and we realize that what we might have previously regarded as a problem can, if handled correctly, become a means to develop our strengths and remove our weaknesses. Whether a situation is a problem or a gift depends on our perception. The choice is ours.

∞ 3 ∞

Meditation as Education

Spiritual education leads us back to the understanding and the experience of our holistic existence as human beings, to the knowledge that we are spiritual—as well as physical, mental, and emotional—beings. Until the spiritual element is acknowledged, the compassion of human nature cannot be realized.

A true spiritual education could be described as:

- learning from others
- growing through others
- integrating with others
- contributing to others.

When we are genuinely learning, only then can we experience spiritual growth. When we grow, we integrate with others; and it is in that integration that there is a natural and mutual contribution to the nature and being of each other. These four processes of education are constantly at work, but they only happen in a way that is enjoyable and meaningful when the spiritual resources of the self are activated and creatively used.

These resources, in conjunction with the mind and intellect, enrich the way we see the world, the way we interact with it, and the way we individually create our place in it. These resources are the original qualities of the self, which we have not properly used for a long time. With the awareness of our spiritual dimension, we start to harness and use these positive energies.

In order to initiate and further sustain this process we need faith in the self:

- Do I believe who I am?
- Do I believe what I have?
- Do I believe I can be more?

Our original resources are, very simply, peace, love, purity, knowledge, and happiness. In Raja Yoga meditation, these are called the five original qualities of the soul. When we return our consciousness to these five qualities and remember them, then we can translate them as follows:

Love: I care and I share.

Peace: I harmonize and I reconcile.

Purity: I respect and I honor.

Knowledge: I am and I exist.

Happiness: I express and I enjoy.

To understand and remember these qualities, we need to recognize the heavy deep shadows which have blotted them out or polluted them. Sometimes we don't recognize the pollutants, because they have ingrained themselves so deeply into the personality that we say "I am this."

We do not realize that we are more than the limits we repeatedly place on ourselves.

What is it that limits and overshadows us? The prayers and the requests of the human race for many centuries. With "I need," "I want," and "I own," people try to place value on the self by relating to the material, external aspects of their lives. However, this does not work; and when people insist on behaving in this way (that is, relating to the outside), then addictive attachments are created. They try to fill themselves, but the exact opposite happens: the self becomes more and more empty. Unfortunately, the mechanism of need and greed functions in this way: first, there is the illusion of gain; secondly, when this is not realized, depletion, instead of enrichment, occurs. Whatever the addiction is, no matter how camouflaged it may be, it quietly but surely ruins the person. It is a silent illness that only meditation can cure.

"I expect" is the great illusion, which converts itself into demanding rights without due respect for others.

Anger in all its forms is a direct result of an expectation not being fulfilled; it brings cries (albeit sometimes silent ones) of "They should have done this," "Why did this happen?" or "Don't you know better?" Disappointment, accusations, and demands are violent energies, which we throw around very naturally and easily in our daily life when our expectations are not fulfilled. They are like a burning fire that eats away at our original spiritual qualities, turning them to a dust that pollutes the self and others.

Instead, let us continue to practice returning our thoughts to the self and remembering our original source of peace. In that experience of deep, natural peace, we will find balance and clarity and the ability to tolerate and adjust to the unexpected.

One of the keys of meditation practice is to quickly gather our thought energy and take it inside to connect to our original qualities, no matter what may be happening outside—or even inside!

> *Let me disconnect from the external and plug in to the internal energies that support me.*

Meditation, in practice, means to enter, and re-enter, this reservoir of peace whenever we need to during the course of the day. This exercise increases self-control and prevents the explosions and reactions of anger that drain our strength. The easy method is not to expect but to accept: then tolerance and respect make our life a lot more comfortable.

There may be other shadows and pollutants, but usually our pain pivots on these: "I own," "I need," "I want," "mine," and "I expect." If we learn to recognize the characteristics of such a consciousness, we are in a position to diffuse difficult situations and thoughts before they overwhelm us. We simply have to remain awake, and then that state of alertness stops these shadows from overpowering us and making us unconscious.

Our needs and wants are truly fulfilled in a healthful way by tuning in to the original resources of the soul, because their fulfilment is not dependent on anyone or anything from outside. When we sustain ourselves from the inside, then our well-being is secure and progressive. As a result, when we express and show our original qualities of self to others, whether it is peace, happiness, or love, they naturally increase inside. The more we give unconditionally, the more we have. This miracle of "quality being" is the consequence of natural purity, the original state of selflessness, which God always has and yogis aspire to return to.

∽ 4 ∾

Touching the Core

MEDITATION IS AN ATTEMPT TO FIND THE TRUE SELF. It is this self that holds the identity of what I am, an identity that, when realized, gives fulfilment and direction to our lives. This is what we call the consciousness of "I am," which emerges in meditation when there is concentration on the present and we focus on the now of "I am," rather than the past or the future ("I was" or "I will be").

To remind us of this state, we use the word "Om," which means "I am a soul," the spiritual identity that acts as a key to human consciousness. As we find and realize the true self, we become aware of the false self and how deeply entrenched it is in our lives, both in our ways of thinking and being.

When we understand this illusory self, then we can begin the process of dissolving its negative effects on the self.

The illusory self is made up of desires that, even when fulfilled, fail to add value or a sense of worth to the self. In fact, quite the opposite process happens.

Let us examine some of these illusions and how they give us a mistaken sense of value:

Illusion	Thought	Result
EGO	I know, I am	arrogance, inflexibility, controlling others
ANGER	I expect	force, aggression
ATTACHMENT	I own, It's mine	insecurity, possessiveness, jealousy
GREED	I want, I need	emptiness, wanting, dissatisfaction
LUST	I desire	exploitation, misuse, emotional dependence

These are the five fires that burn away the quality of human life: uncontrolled emotions that once, in their original pure state, gave happiness and peace to the individual but now create only emptiness and sorrow.

Ego

Identification with the ego and the external creates a false identity and extremes of feeling inferior, or superior, depending on the circumstances and people. It brings with it the thought of "I am," which is based on gender, religion, nationality, achievement, or talent, creating an attachment to the self, which always compares and competes with others. This insecurity leads a person into compelling others to act and think in the same way. Difference is measured as a threat, rather than as an innate gift with a right to expression.

Where there is such ego, only "yes" people are allowed to come close: anyone with a difference of opinion is rejected. With ego, the original uniqueness of the self is denied, unrecognized, and buried deep in the layers of wrong identity. This is why, these days, there is such an identity crisis: humanity has lost its soul—or rather has sold its soul to external "quick fixes," traditions, and attractions.

With ego, there is the idea of "I know best" and consequently the misconceived duty and right to control and manipulate others, in their best interests! This has resulted in dogmas and laws, which fossilize the creativity and uniqueness of others.

"Who am I?" and "What am I?" are questions whose answers lie in the recognition of our inner values and those resources being used in life. When individual human beings find their spiritual identity again, then they adopt the true values of the self, the true being, that cannot be invented or created; they are there all the time but we simply have to remember them.

Through meditation, the pollution of the selfish ego is gradually replaced by the remembrance and the experience of the pure self: the "I" that is not attached to anything or anyone, but is completely whole within itself. The expression of this pure entity is not selfish but selfless, and the person begins to share—where necessary, facilitating the awakening of the true potential of others, just like sunlight. Light is a great facilitator. It steps in, awakens, and moves on. An egoless person acts, interacts, and expresses himself/herself in this way.

Anger

It is easy to understand how anger is one of the greatest fires in the human mind. Anger may take the form of yelling, shouting, and verbal abuse, such as threatening, accusing, demanding, or passing ultimatums: "Do it or else!" But anger is also seen in irritation when we do not speak: it is that silent smoldering where we emit fumes and fires of stored resentments and indignation, which effectively cuts real communication with others and ultimately ruins relationships. We get angry because we expect a certain type of behavior from someone and, when it is not forthcoming, we become violent, convincing ourselves that others deserve to be punished as a result. However, this result is an unresolved violence, which keeps emerging according to time and circumstance. Angry people feel too self-justified to even contemplate forgiving, or letting go, in order to pacify a person or situation—they are too attached to their sense of being right and the other wrong.

In its original form, anger was not anger, not a negative reaction: rather, it was the energy of a positive response to people and situations; but the response gave way to reaction. When we return to our spiritual identity, we begin to rediscover that capacity to be still, or centered, and we are then able to respond positively even to negative situations or people. With spiritual consciousness, the energy of this response is transformed into being able to accept, understand, and deal wisely and peacefully with whoever, or whatever, is encountered.

Attachment

Influenced by the ego, the original power of pure love changes its expression to attachment. In this stage of attachment, we find ourselves trying to possess others or to find an identity through them. In the name of love, we glue ourselves to other people, to roles, to positions, striving to find a sense of security and support. However, because these things are external, there is the underlying fear of loss and this creates more clinging, jealousy, and possessiveness.

Greed

When we turn to the motive and false assumption behind greed, we recognize the thought and feeling that "the more I have, the more I am." It is a combination of trying to add to the value of the self through material possessions, position, role, talent, or achievements, and then becoming attached to these as a form of identity, inevitably leading to personal collapse. To try to add to the sense of self in this way has the effect of detracting from the real self, which is why, in many cases, a person who has everything material is left with the feeling of being empty, disoriented, and even fearful.

We cannot accumulate, or rely on the external, to create a sense of personal value.

People often try to fill the void of personal inadequacy through greed, but this "method" goes against natural, universal laws. All that I am, all that I can be, all that will make me truly happy must begin from inside the self. We have to start from the inside out, not the other way around; otherwise we create desires that have no end, like the seven-headed monster guarding the Golden Fleece: every time Jason, the hero, cut off one head, another grew in its place. The monster did not die until Jason aimed for the heart. Desires are created from wanting one thing or another, believing that we will find achievement when those desires are fulfilled. This pattern of behavior keeps deceiving us, and the proof of this is seen in the state of discontentment and emptiness people find themselves in.

Lust

The desire that many find most difficult to understand is that of lust. This is manifested when the procreative power of the human soul becomes a selfish fire that burns away self-respect and respect for others. People have begun to accept this type of desire as normal, to believe that they may give in to this desire at any time, forgetting that inner qualities like loyalty, patience, and the willingness to grow and learn with another form the basis for a relationship. The undisciplined use of this procreative energy indicates a deep selfishness, which creates and sustains an emotional dependence that damages and often destroys self-value and the spiritual meaning of respectful relationships.

In Raja Yoga meditation, these five diseases of the soul are known as Maya, which means illusion, a deception of the self in pursuing wrong ways to achieve happiness. The human soul has the capacity to follow this path of illusion, or to choose a way of life that is more positive and fulfilling. The choice depends on the degree to which the soul recognizes these five diseases and their progeny and transforms them.

Having recognized the weaknesses, what is the medicine to bring the soul back to a state of good health?

To conquer *ego*, humility and honesty are required. We need the courage to look into the self honestly and acknowledge that the characteristics of "I know" and "I control" exist and have to be removed, if there is to be truth and happiness. We need to remember the original "I am," what we call "Om Shanti" consciousness.

I am a peaceful, spiritual being; this is my true identity.

In order to extinguish *anger*, one has to use peace and silence, to understand that peace is the original state of one's being, to remember that "I am a peaceful being" means to emerge the consciousness of non-violence. Silence—that is, learning to put a brake on the mind and tongue—helps us to think before speaking and consequently saves us from many confrontations with others.

To overcome *attachment*, there needs to be detachment, that is, a space between myself and my violent emotions, desires, and needs, and between myself and others. We need to create a respectful space; to understand that we do not progress or find our selves through others. When we free the self from such a state, then we find our true self and experience a spiritual independence that is kind, loving, and embracing toward others, but simultaneously beyond dependence.

To fill the space created by *greed,* let the soul understand the power of true generosity. The act of repeatedly taking is a disease of selfish need that becomes such a habit that the soul thinks it is normal, especially in relation to other people. Though it may have become normal, it is *not* natural; the proof of this is the pain, sorrow, and discontentment experienced in most people's lives.

Generosity means to give to the self by recognizing the original spiritual qualities of the self, emerging them, and naturally sharing them with others.

To diminish the fire of *lust,* let the soul use the medicine of respect. Where there is a genuine respect for the other, there will not be exploitation of emotions. With respect, balance and harmony cool the senses and the spirit. There is a caring that truly takes into consideration the existence of the other as an independent and valuable being, not to be misused emotionally or physically, by being self-centered.

Raja Yoga means to become the king of the self.

It is through this inner conquest that we are able to recognize and use our immortal resources or medicine. Often, if we cannot unlock or recognize this inner medicine, then the connection with the Supreme Source of energy is necessary. Meditation is the connection with God; it releases these positive energies in the self.

༒ 5 ༒

The Invisible Factor

THE MOST POWERFUL THINGS ARE INVISIBLE. For example, the roots of a tree cannot be seen; they are underground, silently nurturing the visible tree. A house is supported by its foundation deep within the earth; if the foundation is weak, the building will fall when there is some kind of strong pressure, like an earthquake. The essence of matter is the atom; it holds a tremendous amount of energy but cannot be seen with the naked eye.

Can we see God? I have not met anyone who has seen Him. People have experienced or felt God's presence, but no one has actually seen a personal form; yet millions believe in such a Being! In the same way, when it comes to knowing the true self, we ask: "What does the soul look like? Where is it situated?"

A human being is soul and body, spirit and matter, working together cooperatively. The body is like the hardware of a computer, and the spiritual energy, the soul, is a tiny chip of light, where all things are recorded; the full program of the soul is there. When we go into introspective silence, it is in this chip of light, which is actually a point of light energy, that we can remember and rediscover.

The tiny chip of invisible light starts to work effectively when it plugs in to its original consciousness and reactivates those original qualities that enable the soul to work and express itself naturally. The connection is achieved through the power of concentrated thought; this is called "consciousness of the soul." The process of experiencing "soul consciousness" is carried out in meditation: gathering all the thoughts of the mind, creating one concentrated thought, and very gently turning inward in order to make the connection with the original self, the soul.

To take those first steps in gathering the thoughts, we use the positive consciousness of "I am," or what is called "Om Shanti" consciousness. "Om" means "I am," with the deeper meaning that "I am a soul." With this awareness, there comes the experience of one's original spiritual identity.

The soul has five primary qualities; we could say they are the primary colors of our humanity with which we paint the picture of our lives. They are:

Peace

This is the original quality of the soul. Peace is serenity, the personal inner state of nonviolence. In this state of peace, I harmonize with everything and everyone around me. The word "shanti" means peace, and this is the thought we use as the key step in meditation.

Purity

A state of honesty and cleanliness where I am the same inside and outside, not deceiving either myself or others. Consequently, there is no room for artificiality. Purity is the state of original truth where no violence is committed against others, nor can violence be perpetrated against me. When the self is in its original purity, others cannot damage or destroy it, even if they try, because there is a natural aura of protection that acts as an invisible barrier. When I achieve this level of purity, it means I respect all things.

Love

Perhaps the most difficult original quality to achieve, because it has become so mixed up with attachment, possessiveness, and dependence, deeply ingrained habits that have become accepted as normal. As a result, the human being finds it difficult to realize the true form of pure love, which is unconditional. The quality of love means I care, I share, and, in particular, I liberate. True spiritual love never creates that need, or dependency, where others cannot find, or be, themselves. Love is the greatest power and blessing in the universe.

Knowledge

To know and to be what I am eternally and truly, and to exist in this consciousness, is what is meant by knowledge. It is not knowing *about* the soul, peace, love, and so forth, but rather knowing is to *be* the soul, to *be* peace, to *be* love. This quality of true knowing is expressed through "I am," the original awareness of the self that exists beyond the false self of ego.

Happiness

Happiness is the natural expression of joy in being alive and interacting with others. Happiness is only possible when I relate to myself and express respectfully what I am and allow others to share in what I am and what I have. I relate to people and nature and experience the fulfillment of human life through relationship.

As we become aware of these five primary qualities, we gradually realize that each of them has many characteristics.

For example, we understand that love does not mean just a special feeling for one or two people. Spiritual love is far greater: it means respect, tolerance, forgiveness, compassion, and flexibility; there is a universal feeling of belonging, an openness of heart, a generosity of spirit that is all-embracing.

Learning to Meditate

If we do not exercise or use the muscles of our legs for a long time, it will be difficult to use them to walk. This is what has happened to the human spirit. The legs of the mind and intellect have not been exercised spiritually for a long time, and so they have become unhealthy: there is no permanent peace, happiness, or contentment. We have exercised ourselves intellectually by analyzing, discussing, and accumulating information and so forth, but the spiritual dimension has been missing. This has resulted in the soul remaining underdeveloped and undernourished, a real poverty of spirit, which reflects itself in the crises that are happening everywhere, both personally and globally.

> *So, meditation is that spiritual exercise which revives the original qualities of the human soul, bringing them back into our awareness.*

Step 1. Sit in a comfortable and relaxed position. There is no need for a special position, but you need a balance between being too comfortable (in which case it is easy to fall asleep) or too rigid (in which case it is possible that you will begin to feel tense, physically and mentally). Keep the eyes open a little, as this helps us to stay awake; gently concentrate on the third eye.

Step 2. Concentrate your attention on the center of the forehead. Visualize a point of energy. This point of light is the "Om."

> *I am the spiritual identity working within this physical body, my material instrument, but I am not this body. I truly am this tiny point of spiritual energy.*

Step 3. Focus on the thoughts.

> *I am a soul, a spiritual being. I am a point of energy that is eternal and ultimately beyond time, sound, and matter.*

Step 4. Take your thoughts deeper into your inner world. Discover and begin to experience your original strength of peace.

> *My original strength and original quality is peace.*

Step 5. Ask yourself "*What is peace?*" When we examine what it is, then this understanding makes it easy for concentration to take place. If we do not exercise this word in our mind and intellect, it cannot be ingested. Otherwise, we know of the idea of peace but it remains just an intellectual idea rather than a personal reality or experience.

Peace has a number of synonyms, which all have slightly different shades of meaning:

- **Serenity:** The feeling of contentment and being completely full with no need for further additions to the self; a feeling of satisfaction, of wholeness of the self.

- **Calmness:** There are no disturbances or waves in the mind, like a pool of water that is clear and still with not even a ripple to disturb it.

- **Tranquility:** This is the state of harmony in nature and in ourselves that keeps everything in balance naturally.

- **Quietness:** In this state, there are no sounds of uncontrolled thoughts jumping around like a monkey in the mind; our thoughts become essenceful, returning

to the point, with no expansion; it is an economy of
thinking that creates quietness.

- **Stillness:** There is no movement of thoughts. I remain
absorbed in one thought and, in the stillness of silence,
I am at rest, with a feeling of complete detachment
from everything.

Peace has the meaning of harmony, balance, order, and freedom: when
we are free from waste and negativity, then we exist fully serene, fully at
peace with everything.

> *Peace is my original energy and treasure and with concentrated thought I step inside and experience it.*

When we create a thought, it is usually expressed through words and
action. However, during meditation, the thought is held in the mind and
channeled inward; such concentrated thought becomes like a key that
opens up our inner spiritual reservoir.

Now, let's do a meditation exercise:

> *I sit relaxed and concentrate on the center of my forehead,
> very slowly creating thoughts of peace.*

(It is important when meditating not to go too quickly, but rather
to be slow. The slowness allows for depth and ease. Relax the body in a
comfortable position and gently, very gently concentrate on the center
of the forehead).

Continue with these thoughts:

I relax. Slowly I relax. I concentrate on the center of my forehead. I am calm. I begin my journey inward—my journey into silence. In this silence, the mind concentrates on one thought—the thought of the original self, the spiritual self.

Who am I? . . . Gently, I begin to experience the eternal being within. . . . Om . . . I am. . . . I am a spiritual being, . . . a soul; . . . shanti, . . . a being of peace. . . . Peace is my original strength. . . . I, the soul, . . . a point of eternal energy, . . . I am the essence of peace. . . . Peace is harmony. . . . Peace is balance. . . . Peace is serenity. . . . Content, . . . complete, . . . full. . . . As my thought, so my consciousness. . . . Let me remain in this thought: . . . Om shanti. . . . Peace and silence. . . . Peace and silence. . . . I remain still. . . . I focus on myself, . . . as a point of eternal energy. . . . I, the soul, . . . a being of peace, . . . a being of serenity. . . . I remain still. . . . I remain in complete peace: . . . Om shanti.

Remember to do this exercise slowly, giving yourself time when you are not in a hurry. The mind and thoughts may go in other directions; but gently refocus them to realize the "Om Shanti" consciousness, the original consciousness of peace.

Like learning a language, meditation requires systematic and patient practice on a daily basis to receive true benefit. If it is only done once in a while, or only in a state of need, then the state of being peaceful is not easily achieved. Rarely is anything learned, or mastered, immediately. Therefore, it is important not to give up, even if it does not seem to be working. Just keep trying, and gradually it will come by itself. Set aside 15 minutes in the morning and in the evening to practice this; as it becomes easier to do, then you can increase the amount of time.

∾ 6 ∾

The Inner Eye

PEOPLE HAVE ALWAYS BEEN INTRIGUED BY THE CONCEPT OF THE "THIRD EYE." What is it? Can it be opened by having an operation, or by going to places like Tibet or India? In meditation, we understand that the "third eye" means the ability to understand and to perceive correctly and then, on the basis of that perception or insight, to act and behave accordingly. In other words, on the basis of spiritual truths, we think, speak, and act so that peace and well-being become natural in our life.

> *Spiritual values, or truths, are necessary for genuine improvement of the human condition.*

The third eye is the intellect of the soul; when it is open, there is realization of the need to improve, change, and/or create something that will help the self and others to sustain a better quality of life.

The soul has three faculties: the mind through which we create thoughts; the intellect with which we understand, discern, and decide; and the sanskars, which are impressions in the form of memories, personality characteristics, and habits. All three work together: the mind is influenced by both external and internal factors, which can be either positive or negative. The intellect has to understand, discern, and decide what something means and then act. If the intellect is unclear or confused, then understanding and decisions are faulty and, consequently, actions and behavior result in a lot of negativity, both for the self and others.

Throughout history, teachers have come to give spiritual knowledge, through which they attempt to awaken people's consciousness in order to make relationships, attitudes, thoughts, and actions more positive and loving. For this to happen, there has to be a "click" in the intellect, that is, a realization and willingness to change old habits and negative personality characteristics and to become a better human being, ethically and spiritually.

Change is the result of the third eye opening.

In English, there is the word "scope": a wide range of things that can be done, or understood. According to the *Chambers Essential English Dictionary*, "If there is scope for something in a particular set of circumstances, there is freedom, or the opportunity to act in a certain way." When the "third eye" opens, its scope becomes broader and then there is greater possibility to think and act in a more positive way.

Our intellect has become dwarfed by ego, attachments, fear, stress, worry, and greed, to name but a few of our subtle obstacles. However, as we begin to use the wider "scopes" of the third eye in meditation, we are gradually released from a narrow way of thinking and from focusing unduly on wrong things; the more we open up on a subtle level, the more positive and beneficial becomes our focus.

What Kinds of "Scopes" Are There?

There are telescopes, microscopes, periscopes, stethoscopes, and kaleidoscopes. When the intellect is used with a variety of "scopes," then its understanding adapts to the situations it observes. It understands clearly what something really means, and then it discerns what is required for that situation, person, or self and acts accordingly. For any of the "scopes" to work, we need spiritual knowledge as well as meditation. Spiritual knowledge, which is the foundation of any meditation technique, lubricates the intellect and gives it the ability to focus in a variety of ways for a variety of purposes.

Let us take a closer look at the types of "scope" and their impact on our vision.

1. Telescope

When the intellect, or third eye, is used in this way, it is able to understand the reality of "consequence." Every thought, every word, and every action is like a planted seed that, in time, will bear fruit. When there is realization of this reality, then there is attention paid as to how we think, speak, and act. We realize the importance of our own responsibility in creating certain situations, in creating our own attitude and state of mind; there is greater care and a more responsible use of our own power of choice.

> *With telescopic vision, we become the knower of the three aspects of time.*

In Raja Yoga, this is called being *trikaldarshi,* which literally means having the "vision of the three aspects of time" in the sense that from the present I create my future, and from the present I can learn from the past; the past cannot be changed, but my attitude to what has happened can be changed. Therefore, rather than having regret or bitterness, I understand the lessons of life and move on.

2. Microscope

When the lens of the intellect becomes refined, then it is able to examine many things in detail. In the same way that a microscope is able to detect bacteria and the types of germ that cause particular types of disease, so too is the intellect able to use its microscopic capacity to detect those germs that cause emotional and spiritual illness. For example, it is able to examine and understand that the illness of anger comes from the germ of expectation, that the illness of possessiveness comes from the germ of insecurity, that the illness of aggression, or forcefulness, comes from the germ of fear, and that the illness of stress stems from the germs of worry, doubt, and greed. If the germs are seen and understood, then the illness can be cured through the application of appropriate knowledge and meditation.

> *Meditation, in the form of a focused silence, acts like a spiritual laser, dissolving the acquired germs and emerging the original healing energies of the self, such as peace and self-respect.*

Without this focused silence, it is difficult to remove the germs, even if they are seen and understood. The original innate energy of the soul is needed for any permanent cure.

3. Periscope

This is the ability of the intellect to come out, observe, understand, and initiate appropriate action and, when necessary, go back inside and be calm and still. This act of taking the thoughts inside is called introspection; in this introspective state, the self can re-energize, examine, reflect, and refine, or just be completely still—whatever it may wish to do in that state of silence. When the intellect uses its capacity as a periscope, it is able to find a balance between the inside and outside worlds.

Effective meditation means to gather the positive resources of the inner self and then use them in the outer world.

It is important to remain neither too much inside nor too much outside, but constantly to create a balance between the inner and outer realities. Meditation resembles the cyclic path of energy: going from the inside out and then from the outside in, gathering information or experiences that we need to reflect on or understand better. On other occasions, it may be a question of recharging our minds with positivity and peace: we go inside and, with the practice of silence, the battery becomes re-energized.

4. Stethoscope

This is the intellect being so sensitively focused that it can recognize the realities behind appearances. Sometimes we call this intuition. To be intuitive often means that the third eye is able to tune in to the hidden silent vibrations of other people and situations. Vibrations are energies, which are constantly being transmitted by all things, particularly living things and people. A person may not say anything, or may even say the opposite of what he or she is feeling; but we are able to understand this contradiction, either through facial expressions or body language, or by picking up the thoughts.

The doctor uses the stethoscope to "hear" the body of the patient and to examine and understand the pulse and rhythm of the body in order to gauge the health of the person; it is like a third ear!

If the intellect wishes to understand the pulse of another person, in order to truly cooperate and help properly, then it has to have the capacity of a third ear, which means developing the art of really listening and catching the needs of the situation and person. When the intellect is used like a stethoscope, it needs to be very introspective, very concentrated, and very open. In this way, the intellect is used like a third eye and a third ear; seeing and listening become the same thing and such perception brings creative and constructive assistance to the many illnesses that now plague the human spirit.

5. Kaleidoscope

A kaleidoscope creates beautiful patterns from chaotic bits and pieces, which are scattered everywhere; when the kaleidoscope is turned, disorder becomes order, chaos becomes beauty and symmetry. The drama of life is constantly turning and we are part of its cyclic movement; sometimes this cyclic movement of life is supportive, comprehensible, and enjoyable; at other times, it is tense, fearful, stressful, and incomprehensible. There is confusion and fear because we do not understand what is happening, why it is happening, and how it will get better. Things not only appear chaotic but also hopeless. If the intellect is able to go beyond the questions of "Why?" "What?" and "How?" and just be still, without judgments or pressure, for some period of time, then things do work out. To do this requires faith.

> *The power of faith means that we know that, somehow and somewhere, right solutions and answers will come in their own time.*

We are so used to controlling people and situations to obtain a particular result that we have forgotten how to use this power of faith.

Faith says "Plant the right seeds, make the right effort, but also let things be." Faith does not mean we should be passive, but rather that we should have acted and thought about something, and to then have the patience and trust that the Drama of Life is also taking care of it; the outcome of any action is not just up to me.

In Raja Yoga meditation, we often hear the term "a faithful intellect is victorious." As the Drama of Life turns, such an intellect works like a kaleidoscope and can perceive the beautiful patterns, often hidden, that in time become visible and benevolent.

Success, or victory, depends as much on doing the task with the right intention as it does on allowing things to take their own course. Wisdom is an awareness of this balance.

❧ 7 ❧

Knowledge and Truth

THE FIRST STEP INTO EXPERIENCE, particularly the meditation experience, is knowledge. What does it mean to "know"? Knowing involves four steps, which ultimately give the meditator the experience of realization:

- The first step of knowing is **information**. With information, our intellect opens to new ideas and opinions. To be properly informed, we need to listen carefully.

- The second step of knowing is **knowledge**, when we begin to reflect on and think about the ideas and views that we have listened to. At this point, we often have to select only a few of the ideas we have heard, as it is not always feasible to reflect on all the information that is fed to us. In order to deepen our understanding, we reflect on the information and sometimes discuss our findings and thoughts with others.

- The third step of knowing is when we move from thinking to doing—that is, from knowledge to **wisdom**.

Wisdom is gained when we commit ourselves "to doing." Knowledge, translated into our everyday behavior, is called wisdom, which in turn is called quality life. A life of quality is where personal values are not only realized but also lived and experienced through our practical actions.

- Doing, or practice, naturally brings us to the fourth and final step of knowing, which is called **truth**.

Truth is "to be": the pure state of being where nothing needs to be added, where nothing can be subtracted.

For a human being, this takes a long time and a variety of processes. It is the ultimate state of consciousness that yogis and meditators aspire to. (This is often referred to as the consciousness of "Om.") It is said that God is eternally in this state of truth. "Om" is the consciousness of "I am," the consciousness that denotes both an uncreated selfhood and a pure state of being. The human soul originally had this consciousness of "Om," but gradually forgot it. Therefore, the aim of "knowing" (or at least *spiritual* knowing) is to return to this original state. The way of return is called "remembrance": that is, to pay attention and keep remembering the eternity of the self, otherwise referred to as the soul, the *atma*.

On a spiritual path, we always need these four steps; but there is a great temptation for the majority of people to stay on the first two, which involve listening and thinking. Without a systematic and consistent commitment to personal action, we just develop the art of conceptualizing, philosophizing, and discussing. Moreover, without practice and silence we cannot develop the inner strength that is so vital for everyday life.

One aim of meditation is to develop inner strength through attention to practice.

Practice is to observe and to take the opportunity to transform knowledge into an experience that helps us in our daily life.

One aspect is the practice of values such as tolerance, patience, and flexibility. Another is for the meditator actually to experience the highest level of consciousness. It is said that when this highest level of consciousness is attained, there is the strength to practice those values that create well-being.

How can we go beyond these stages of information, knowledge, and even wisdom to experience the original state of being: that is, truth?

One way to describe the process is to compare it to the game of the pole-vaulter. The pole-vaulter has a long pole to help jump over the barrier. The athlete runs for a short distance, and then quickly fixes the end of the pole into the ground, enabling the body to be lifted up. When the athlete reaches a certain point in the air, the very pole that was used to get to that point is discarded: if the athlete fails to let go of the pole, then the body will be propelled backward and it will be impossible to accomplish the task of jumping over the barrier.

The same mechanism is involved when a person wishes to attain realization of the self and an experience of a higher state of consciousness. To experience realization, we have to run some distance, collecting the necessary information. Then we use the pole of knowledge and wisdom to lift us off the ground of ordinary consciousness. But we must then let go of the very knowledge that we used to elevate our minds, and take a jump of faith, flying over the barrier of "ordinary consciousness" to experience a new and higher level of consciousness. If there is no faith, then there is not enough trust to let go and jump.

Many people do not let go of the pole of knowledge and, as a result, fall into the spinning of speculation and the habit of analysis and discussion; the experience of spiritual consciousness eludes them. The pull of the ego draws the consciousness back to the ground. The irony is that, thinking they have jumped over the barrier, they regard themselves as being in the privileged position of knowing. Then they think that from this privileged position, they have the prerogative of judging and being better than those who "know" in a different way.

The ones who have let go of the pole can be characterized by their wide, creative perspective and their benevolent strength.

Ultimately, true knowing is a state of positive being and its most powerful experience and expression is in silence.

8

The Power of Silence

IT SEEMS CONTRADICTORY TO SPEAK OR WRITE ABOUT SILENCE, because silence is really something that needs to be experienced. In the experience of silence, we discover deep spiritual truths and come to know our spiritual selves. Silence grows within us, helping us to progress and develop in a very subtle way, just like a seed: the flower is hidden in the seed, and the seed is hidden in the earth. Sunlight touches the earth, which warms the seed, and the flower begins to grow.

Like a seed, we are also full of a great deal of potential. It is not really knowledge, or discussion, that will truly develop that potential. They help, of course, but it is the light of silence that penetrates very deeply and awakens the potential within, inspiring it to burst into flower. Silence is also a space that gives the mind oxygen, allowing the creation of something new, filling life with power and strength.

Everybody's religion nowadays is one of being busy. Everyone rushes around, doing something, proving something, showing something. In that rush to be someone, we tend to forget the great power and miracle found in stillness.

One aspect of meditation is that it teaches us to face life from the inside.

It takes us to that point of stillness where we find the strength to change and heal the inner self. In that silence, we are able to find perspective and insight. In a deep state of introspection, we clearly observe our thoughts, seeing our true motives; when we understand that our intentions are perhaps not quite right, then we are in a position to say to ourselves: "Hold on a minute!"

When we use silence to check our thoughts at that level, then we begin to realize that many of the things we are thinking about are not really worth thinking about. At this point, we become spiritually economical, which in fact leads us to becoming very generous. A lot of precious energy is lost, both mentally and emotionally, on wasteful and negative thinking. Ninety-five percent of our time is wasted on thinking about others; we go on and on with a string of expectations, which becomes like a hammer of demand on other people's heads. Take a combination of expectations and demand, and what does it equal? Conflict!

When we learn to become silent and to reflect on our inner selves, we start feeling satisfied with what we find inside, and there is a deep sense of contentment.

We become more compassionate in our outlook and start accepting others for who they are. The more we are able to accept, the sooner we find that there is harmony in our relationships. We start saving energy, sparing our thoughts and our words. This is accompanied by more patience, tolerance, flexibility, easiness, and lightness. Silence teaches us the art of living. Silence can be misused to isolate oneself, sure; but true, positive silence gives us a balance between our inner and outer worlds. Having explored our inner self, we collect our positive energy, become aware of our positive qualities, and then very naturally these are expressed externally. We move our concentration to the inner self and then to the external world. Then we go inwards again. It is a circular movement. As we go into silence, we recharge our inner energies, become one with the self, heal the self, relax, and release the self from negativity. We accrue so many benefits by simply stepping inside to meet our true selves. As we draw out these riches and resources, what do we do with them? We share them and give them out; and in doing this, we receive and we learn.

Silence is the guiding light that helps us to find a balance between inner and outer expression.

Too much silence is not good. We need to go in, discover, and then come out and share. If we only stay inside, we can lose the self. We can become uncaring about others. That is not a healthy silence. Then again, you get those who always remain with the external. They spend all their time criticizing, analyzing, discussing, examining, rushing around. They cannot be still for even a few moments.

One of the methods we use in Raj Yoga is called "Traffic Control." This method consists of being still for a few moments, stopping the traffic of our thoughts. Stepping back for a few moments, we free the self from tension. We look at the picture of where we are going and then step back into whatever activity we were involved in. However, going into that brief silence actually helps us to be more effective and more functional. This is a very effective method, particularly when practiced a few times a day.

Meditation actually helps us to discover our real self.

This is something that most people have a problem with nowadays; they don't know who exactly they are, or where they are going, or why they are here. They lead a very robotic existence (eating, sleeping, working, drinking, and so forth). Eventually, they get frustrated and break down. Unfortunately, in today's world, there are many economic, social, and political breakdowns. These arise from crises in people, due to the diminishing prominence of values in everyday life. Moreover, people have such misplaced values: wanting, needing, taking, and comparing. All this takes them away from their simplicity and their naturalness. How can we help them to get back to their roots? By leading them to silence, to meditation.

The word "meditation" comes from the Latin word "meditari," which is a probable cognate of the word "mederi," meaning "to heal." Journeying inside, discovering the inner self and our true power, is the beginning of the healing process, in which we are able to put back all the broken pieces with a lot of love. Do I like, respect, and love myself? In meditation, I reconcile myself to myself, I accept myself, I discover the uniqueness of my own being at this particular point in time. I also tune in to those original resources of my spirit, which are simply love, peace, joy, and happiness, to name but a few.

With patience and practice, we need to strengthen three aspects of our real selves:

- self-respect
- self-esteem
- self-confidence

Self-respect

This depends on knowing who I am, knowing my eternal, spiritual self. When I have found that sense of spiritual identity, I feel I have a right to be here, to exist. Without the spiritual dimension, it is difficult to really respect myself deeply. In this case, I base my respect on identifying with the superficial aspects of my being: looks, gender, success, my spouse, my intelligence. With such superficial identification, I will never have a stable sense of self-respect, because people's opinions change. Today they love me, tomorrow they reject me. What is the consequence of depending on their opinions? I will end up fluctuating all the time—feeling positive when they say good things, and feeling down when they say negative things. To stay stable in my self-respect, I need to nurture a deeper understanding of my spiritual identity (the foundation of this being that I am a soul) and tap into those riches that are within me eternally, waiting to blossom, like the flower from the seed.

As I become grounded in such a spiritual awareness, those riches and resources start flowing out of me. The more stable I am in my self-respect and spirituality, the more I emanate what I truly am. I feel a deep sense of contentment and I am happy to be me, however I am. I accept myself as I am. When I have no connection with my spiritual roots, I become dependent on others and, unfortunately, I sometimes mistake this dependence for love when it is normally just a need or an attachment. When this happens, the relationship doesn't work for long, because I have attached myself to someone, giving them neither space nor respect. They begin to feel suffocated because I have trespassed on their freedom and, eventually, the result of the whole relationship is a feeling of bondage. Only when the soul is in a state of complete self-respect can there be freedom in relationships.

Self-esteem

Self-esteem comes when I really value myself. When I place value on myself, then others, too, will value me. When I don't value myself, how can I expect others to value me? If I continually put myself down, saying "I'm no good" or "I am not capable," other people who hear this will start believing it. So what do I do? The key word is "consciousness." As I start to become more conscious, more spiritually alert, then I am in a position to start valuing my life. The effect of this is that I start valuing others, understanding that everyone has their own position: not higher or lower, just different. Each one's uniqueness has its value and when I recognize the value of the self, I develop self-confidence.

Self-confidence

Self-confidence is very much linked to the understanding that I definitely have something to contribute to life through my own uniqueness. Each one of us is unique. That goes without saying. Unless a person has a sense of contributing, or offering, something to life, he or she cannot really be happy. I cannot be happy when I am just taking; it simply doesn't work. I can only be happy when I am sharing and offering the best of myself. In that way, I don't feel depleted. When I offer the best of myself in an unselfish way, my happiness increases: the more I give, the more I receive. We start to understand that the well-being of individuals begins when they can contribute what they are, and what they have, to others. To be a true human being means to have true spiritual powers, like love, peace, and happiness, that are brought into daily life—not just appearing as words or emotions, but truly manifesting themselves in behavior.

For example, take the quality of love. It is not just a feeling of passion, the Hollywood type of love. It is much deeper: it is being able to say "I learned from the past"; it is forgetting grievances; it is forgiveness. Rather than having animosity, or resentment, let me show compassion. The more I feel compassion, the more I love myself. Forgiveness is a wonderful medicine for me because it releases me from feeling bitter. It is also wonderful for the person I forgive. Hatred does not justify anything, nor does it release anyone from pain, or other negative emotions and feelings. Let me learn, forget, and move on. This is a guaranteed therapy.

Love is just one example of the spiritual resources that are found within the self. By tapping into these resources, we become better human beings. It takes a little time to connect with the self in this way, but if we keep this aim clearly in front of us, we will be successful. Practicing meditation helps us to reach our goals, because during meditation we link our soul self with the Supreme Energy, who fills us with power. The freer we become, the more confident we are with the ability to trust our selves more. We become more stable in our own self, we are able to control our reactions a bit better, and we wait. We don't suppress the self. Rather, we wait, observe, clarify, and then control our reaction (including, of course, our tongue!).

> As we start to do things more positively and compassionately, we start to grow in our own self-respect and self-confidence.

We don't want to be ruled by our negative emotions. We still meet them, acknowledge them, try to understand them, and dissolve them. We cannot pretend that they are not there, but we are no longer a slave to the negative. As we follow our spiritual path more closely, we learn that we don't want to damage ourselves, nor do we want to damage others. We become a little more careful. Sometimes we know what the right thing to do is, but still we are not able to control our reactions or act correctly. We know, understand, and agree, but still we can't do the right thing. Then we are filled with guilt and regret, having done the wrong thing. We lose our self-respect. What can we do then? Where do we find the strength to change? In silence.

In silence, we are able to find the strength to be able to put those values into practice. Silence is a great therapy for healing the self. If we remain very quiet and concentrate, we save a lot of outward energy, with the result that we act and speak less. When that energy is saved, then we are able to turn inward and even heal our physical body.

On a daily basis, the mind needs to go into a quiet space for refreshment and reflection, in much the same way as the body needs regular breaks for rest and nourishment. Refreshment occurs when the mind is able to recharge itself: that is, to re-energize and to have the strength to remain positive, light, and creative. Reflection is the time we give ourselves to refine our understanding so that our interaction with others is of the highest quality. Through reflection, we can change the way we think, feel, and interact. We change the way we are voluntarily and without pain.

> *Knowledge without silence is like a bird trying to fly with only one wing.*

Silence empowers an individual's capacities and enables the recognition and release of his or her unique potential. In today's world, silence is as necessary for the mind as oxygen is for the body. We need that spiritual breath that sustains our life in a way that is meaningful and fulfilling.

9

The Seven Steps of Silence

THE SEVEN STEPS OF SILENCE are the complements, the bridges, or steps, that take us into the depths of knowledge, increase our core strength, and release creative energy into the world: a contribution that not only can we all make, but which is of the utmost necessity.

Step One: Listening

People often speak of opening the third eye; but our true step into deepening understanding is to open our third ear! What this means is to tune the self to understand what is really being said.

> *This requires that I create a stillness within, by detaching*
> *as far as possible from the conditionings of my personality,*
> *from myself, and from my way of thinking, so as not to*
> *interpret new knowledge according to old patterns.*

I need to step back from myself in order to listen to myself. Listening is creating that respectful space between myself and the other, which facilitates a real understanding of what the other is trying to say to me. Listening through the "third ear" creates a link of empathy: an attentive calm and openness that focuses the mind so that reality can be grasped. Such attentive awareness enables the mind to create concentrated and pure thought. As Albert Einstein said, "I firmly believe, as the ancients believed, that pure thought can grasp reality."

What is the reason for going into silence? Why would I want to tune my mind and attitude to listening?

As the world becomes more complex and problems become further intertwined, *listening is the first step to communicating and harmonizing with everyone;* it is a method to understand the reality of others in order to live better with them. Listening to myself, to God, to others, and to nature enables the self to harmonize and to enjoy a sense of equilibrium.

Step Two: Reflection

Reflection is a necessary step in digesting knowledge, to show that I understand what I hear.

> *Reflection is an exercise of the mind and intellect that goes into the depths of understanding an idea, or realization, with the intent of practicing it in daily life.*

Values in my life signal that knowledge has been digested; without this, knowledge simply remains a beautiful aspect, appreciated, interesting information in my intellect but without the ability to give me strength because it is still external, it has not been internalized.

All quality action, all newness of perception, all new insights or vision, require a space for silent reflection as a preliminary step. Reflection is the springboard from which we can dive into the pool of quality action.

> *Quality action is that action which is truly appropriate to person, circumstance, and the need of the moment.*

Normally, we are lost in the business of action, its routine, and its ritual that make our life so mechanistic and hence dull and boring, or demanding and hectic.

A mind and intellect that do not give time and attention to reflective silence become lazy, though externally there is lots of activity for hours and hours. No new heights are reached because there is no depth of awareness in what we are doing, no reflection on purpose, nor intention. As a result, we get trapped by routine.

To be dictated to by external situations, which make us run around without stopping internally, induces unnecessary stress on the mind, which keeps us tied to the strings of the external, like a puppet pulled, pressed, and pushed by circumstances.

> *To break free from this force, to relieve the mind of the weight of stress and waste and routine, I need to step inside and reflect on who I am and where I am going and reassess my value system.*

Otherwise, life becomes like a wheel that keeps spinning faster and faster until we become dizzy—we want to get off, but it is going so fast that we do not know how.

Reflection and taking time to understand bring us to the essence of everything.

Step Three: Concentration

When we reflect properly, we start to be economical with our thought energy. When milk is churned, it is gradually reduced in volume until it becomes butter. When we have many ideas or thoughts about a particular thing, and we reflect in the right way, those ideas start to become cleaner and clearer: that is, more essenceful.

Bringing our thoughts to the essence is called concentration.

Such concentration is natural, not forced. We cannot concentrate naturally unless we have been through the reflection process.

When the mind gets to that point of concentration where mental energy is conserved, then we are empowered. An inner spring of energy is opened, which flows through us and takes us up to another level of consciousness.

With some meditation techniques, people are given ideas or mantras, which they often simply repeat. These ideas do not penetrate the mind, bringing any sense of meaning. People bounce them around like a ball in their mind; from the mind, the ball of thought is bounced to the mouth. Sound patterns are repeated, but nothing has really been understood. The result of this is that there is no power generated from within to effect change in behavior, or personality, so everything continues in the same way. In these cases, people are not focused on spirituality. Consequently, after a while, such people find meditation boring: they fall asleep, or they think that by repeating words, either verbally or mentally, they are "doing" meditation. However, the right type of concentration is not brought about simply by the repetition of sounds or ideas.

Natural concentration happens when the mind can hold a thought for a long time, when thoughts are under our own control.

Without concentration the mind goes here, there, and everywhere, jumping like a monkey from branch to branch, idea to idea. When there is a natural concentration, we master our mind and there is peace. This one-pointed concentration on a thought, holding it for as long as we like, gradually accumulates strength in the mind and in the self.

A strong mind is a mind that is peaceful, stable, and contented, and that can remain in the essence of a thought. There is no waste caused by overthinking or speed of thought; these are the two greatest diseases of the mind these days, which is why there is so much stress and mental breakdown.

Step Four: Connection

Once we have mastered the art of concentration, we are able to experience the fourth step of meditation, which is connection. With our power of thought, we connect with our original feelings and state of peace. We plug into our socket and feel the current; as we connect, we experience the fifth step of silence.

Step Five: Absorption

The self is absorbed in spiritual peace. For this connection and absorption to take place, the thought cannot be distracted; otherwise, a short circuit occurs and the energy flow stops because the thought has become disconnected from the socket.

> *If we refine our understanding of the fourth step, the connection in Raja Yoga meditation is not only with the original self but also with God.*

The human soul plugs in to the unlimited pure-energy reservoir of the Universe, often called God. This Being is in reserve throughout eternity; existing beyond time and matter. God is beyond the effect of pollution and decay, which befalls every human soul; therefore, when we need to clean out our system, re-energize, or refill ourselves with power, we have to tap into that Reservoir, and we can only do that through our thoughts.

> *If the thought is concentrated enough, the mind is able to transcend the ordinary, to absorb the qualities of that Being, and to learn the meaning of inner excellence and liberation.*

Accordingly, we concentrate, connect, and absorb pure energy into the self. The deeper the concentration, the greater the absorption in the self of the qualities radiated by God.

Step Six: Filling

As the self absorbs the energy of peace, or whatever positive energy it needs, then it fills itself with that quality completely. If the concentration remains unbroken, then the absorption and filling happen quite naturally and automatically.

Step Seven: Donation

Donating is the final step of silence. We have filled the self with a particular quality, and it starts flowing out of us. We allow this quality to touch the atmosphere around us and consciously donate this vibration to the world, enabling those in need to feel it and absorb it.

> *This is the ultimate step of a true meditator, often referred to as the "lighthouse" state.*

A lighthouse stands still and stable in one position and beams light all around. We are able to bring an original quality of the self into our consciousness; fill ourself with it; and then, very naturally, let it radiate from the mind.

One of the most important aspects in this step of silence is the link with the Supreme Energy. We make this link with the Supreme Source, we absorb from that Source, we fill the self from that Source, and then donate all that the Source has given us.

This is called "angelic" or "instrument" consciousness.

It is said that an angel is a human soul who has fallen so deeply in love with that Source of Light that it has transformed completely. It is totally filled with Light and Peace, and its task is only to serve, to share Divine Love and Peace.

Let us practice the first three steps with an exercise in Raja Yoga meditation.

1. *I hold in my mind the words Om Shanti, "I am a peaceful soul."*

> Let us reflect on this statement, or mantra. A mantra is something that frees the mind from wasteful and negative thoughts, stress, and worry. A mantra is usually repeated over and over again in order to get the desired results. However, in meditation it is not a matter of repeating words over and over again; it is much more important to truly understand them. Otherwise it becomes forced concentration. Concentration of the mind should be natural because when it is, the mind can remain in a state of peace and relaxation for a very long time. The consequence of this is a recharging of the battery of the self, a renewal of energy from inside.

How do we achieve this state of natural concentration on the thought "I am a spiritual being," "I am a peaceful being"?

2. I reflect on "Om," the consciousness of "I am."

What does "I am" mean? In this thought, the attention is drawn only to the present moment. I have no need to go into "I was," "I will be," "I hope to be," or "I should be." To go deep into the self, *I need to be completely in the present.* This thought of "I am" takes me into the consciousness of self-realization.

3. I focus and concentrate on the thought until I stop thinking about it and experience it.

These first three steps of silence are the most important; once mastered correctly, the other four steps follow very easily

∽ 10 ∽

Connecting with the Divine

PLATO ONCE SAID THAT TRUE KNOWLEDGE is to remember what you have forgotten. Truth actually means not to forget, that the human soul carries within itself all the knowledge and resources it needs to lead a happier life.

In Raja Yoga meditation, the word "remembrance" is used, rather than "yoga" or "meditation," when we are trying to describe what meditation actually means and does. Meditation that empowers the self by giving peace to the mind and clarity to the intellect, that brings about positive change to the personality, is not achieved simply through a ritual, or a repetition of words, where there is little, if any, understanding. Rather, it is achieved by understanding what those words mean, reflecting on the ideas carried by those words and, with concentrated thought based on those ideas, bringing them actively into our consciousness. When the consciousness has that enlightened awareness, which is achieved through concentrated silence rather than repetition of sound, then the next step is action. We emerge our original state of peace, of knowing, of love, not just for ourselves but to use and share in daily life.

We cannot experience spiritual powers and values until we understand what they mean and where they come from and decide to apply them in our life.

Understanding and application are the basis of self-realization and positive living.

Of course, what happens is that sometimes we do understand and even apply our values; but, because of the pressures and distractions of life, we forget to apply them consistently or systematically. This is why we need to revise and refresh our understanding and awareness through the practice of meditation every day, especially in the early morning.

How often do we breathe? How often do we eat and drink? To stay alive, these practices must happen consistently and systematically. This principle also applies to spiritual well-being. I cannot maintain my spiritual health unless, on a daily basis, I connect with myself and remember who I am and what I have within myself, recharging the self in the depths of silence.

Each morning before I start the journey of the day, to sit in silence, to reflect, to concentrate, and to experience the consciousness of "Om Shanti" recharges the self for the whole day. When I remember my original state of peace and inner harmony, my mind and intellect create an oasis of stability within, which helps me to face any storms of negativity that arise during the day.

To keep remembering our spiritual identity and our spiritual resources is a challenge. Again and again, we need to remember and to return to our essence, our worth, and our original strength. The words "Om Shanti" are the thoughts that help us remember all this, thoughts that—when gently and slowly spoken in the mind—become a key to opening up our spiritual and human resources.

Even a few times during the day, we can stop for some moments to reflect and remember to be peaceful and silent. This act of stopping is like putting a brake on the mind.

I observe in what direction my thoughts, words, and actions are going and then, if necessary, redirect or keep moving in the same direction with more clarity and focus.

This practice of remembrance is called "traffic control." When we do stop from time to time, it becomes a means to refresh, recharge, and reorient. However, we become so busy, or so action-oriented, that we often forget to stop.

Then the traffic becomes heavy and the driving tense, tiring, stressful, and irritating; our mind and nerves seem ready to explode! To prevent all explosions and emotional eruptions, which ultimately destroy or damage our effectiveness, we need to stop. This is one practical use of remembrance.

On a deeper level, remembrance also means to connect the heart and mind to the Supreme Energy Source of the Universe; through this connection, the self is not only re-energized; it's also liberated from the repetitive patterns of wasteful thoughts and behaviors.

Sometimes one has the best intentions, the sincerest determination to eliminate certain habits. But after a while, these habits always seem to return. We feel trapped, we feel we cannot do what we would like to do, and so we lose hope—or even the will to try again. The link with the Supreme Source of Energy gives the self the power to change, to dissolve, and to finish negative patterns.

This link, which is possible when there is attention filled with love, enables a current of pure energy to reach the self; through this spiritual current, it becomes easier to stabilize in a positive state, because this energy creates permanent changes. This link of love between the soul and the Supreme Source is also called remembrance.

When I remember the One, then the memory of my own state of original being returns and this memory creates the aim to return and rediscover those forgotten—or half-forgotten—qualities of the original being.

The Supreme Source has the power to remind us of what we were, because His original state of being is permanent. He never forgets Himself, is never polluted, and remains eternally true to Himself in the state of spiritual, or soul, consciousness. As a result, He is the blueprint of what we were, of what we are to become. Very simply, the qualities of peace, love, purity, happiness, and truth are there in Him, visible and available to those who wish to tune in and receive.

What we remember, we become; and so it is important to remember the right things. Number one on the list is thoughts of the original self and the Supreme Source.

Imagine two points of light: one here on the earth, in time and matter, and the other beyond the earth, in another world of silence and peace. When these two points connect through the power of thought and feeling, then there is a union that allows for a flow of energy and the experience of our true being. I, the soul, the point, am here, and the Supreme Soul, also a point of light, is up there. However, love and remembrance bring such closeness that there is no feeling of distance or separation.

To achieve remembrance that empowers, we need to plug in every day to the Supreme Source in silence, in a way that is beyond ritual or sound.

It is a personal connection that requires no audience and no rules, only an honest heart. When a person is well-intentioned, the plug of love fits into the socket and the self receives whatever it needs, whatever is useful for it to create and sustain a life of quality.

> *In order to remember to create a quality life, ask the self*
> *"What is my highest ideal?"*

Know it, understand it, follow it, be it, no matter what happens. Remember: I achieve what I believe.

❧ 11 ❧

Eight Principles of Spiritual Living

THERE IS SOMETIMES THE MISCONCEPTION that meditation keeps us in the clouds beyond reality. People frequently think it is an escape. However, for those who meditate appropriately, meditation (that is, the art of listening, reflecting, and concentrating) brings us to a point where we are empowered and therefore able to face life positively and realistically.

Let us take a look at the principles of spiritual living. There are eight fundamental principles that, together with our own reflection and silence, help us practically in daily life.

Principle 1: Observe and Not Absorb

To observe means we take a new mental position in whatever situation, or with whatever relationship, we find ourselves. Observation is a silent skill—a skill we need to learn if we are to assess clearly what positive changes are needed in a particular situation, or in relation to a person. To be a detached observer means to keep the mind clear and free and therefore open to new perspectives as we learn to listen and tune in to the reality of the other.

Being able to observe enables us to be creative, productive, and effective, because we have made space for true and better understanding.

If we fail to learn this art of observing, we are likely to react and absorb ourselves in the negativity of the person or event. We get lost in the quicksand of "What's wrong?", which prevents us from putting things right. As we absorb and fill ourselves with negative emotion, we become heavy and remain helplessly rooted to the ground. The gravity of overload does not allow us to rise above a situation and to perceive the reality of what is happening. As a result, we lose perspective and overreact.

If we wish to understand how the mental position of observation gives us the power of perspective, we can look at the example of the bird and the ant. The ant, extremely busy, running here and there, scrambling over everything in its rush to find and collect food, will see only what is in front of it. The bird, on the other hand, leaves the earth and, as it flies higher and higher, starts to see the bigger picture, compared to when it was on the ground or on the branch of a tree. Seeing the whole picture, it has a completely different perspective. It is only then that it can truly see where to go and what to do.

When we lose perspective, we get too involved in the details, missing the "obvious," and cannot imagine, or think of, other realities.

Principle 2: To Be Aware but Not Judgmental

On the path of Raja Yoga meditation, there is a saying, "See, but don't see! Hear, but don't hear!", which means to remain aware of all realities, including the negative, but not to focus on them. We get caught up in the negative because we react and the reactions manifest themselves as judgments, accusations, criticism, or labeling. We do all this when we feel threatened by what we are unfamiliar with, when we are moved out of our comfort zones. As soon as we judge or criticize, we put everything into convenient boxes and, just as convenience foods are not always so healthful, such mental and attitudinal conveniences are a great danger, because we mentally seal the fate of the person or situation: they are like this and so must be treated accordingly. Unfortunately, this is often done in an unconscious way, which is why Raja Yoga meditation is used to bring such attitudes and behaviors to the surface, conscious awareness.

When our vision and attitude remain judgmental or critical, they do so because there is no input of positivity from the self to encourage or allow a positive change.

There cannot be a positive output when there is a negative input.

We frequently work in this way, wanting others to be better in some way, but, instead of helping them or having faith in them and seeing their good qualities, we hinder them by concentrating on their past, their weaknesses, and their mistakes. Our focus is completely negative, but still we expect them to change for the better!

When our awareness is more detached, rather than focusing on what is wrong, we look at how we can put something right by contributing a positive feeling or attitude. This anonymous and benevolent contribution is a generous act, which offers a solution, instead of the usual complaints proffered by critical and judgmental people.

A spiritually aware person offers remedies and does not indulge in self-righteous complaints.

Maturity means to be fully aware and, to the extent one is aware, to keep silent. Many things work themselves out when our own input is consistently kind and honestly motivated.

Principle 3: Focus and Flow

If we look at the sun and the earth, we appreciate a basic and fundamental law of function, which we as human beings can learn from, that is of paramount help in the right movement of life. By means of light, the sun gives life to the earth; in addition, the sun is fixed in its position to enable the earth and all the other planets of our solar system to continue in their rhythmic, harmonious orbit. Otherwise, there would be chaos, upheaval, and great damage. The earth, on the other hand, constantly moves in repetitive cycles around the sun. This movement allows for change and expression, which have a beginning, middle, and end. In other words, the phenomenon of time is created as a direct result of the earth's balanced and harmonious cyclic rhythms. Both the fixed position of the sun and the movement of the earth are necessary for life. The earth has all the potential for life but, without light from a fixed source, there would be no life. In the same way, the sun has the power to give life, but if the moving earth did not hold the potential, even with light, there would be no manifestation of life.

In certain situations and moments we need focus: that is, a concentration of thought, will, and understanding. These three need to be together in one focused point if we are to reach depth and newness. However, if we become overfocused, then rigidity and pressure gradually set in. This subsequently leads to an imbalance that makes us lose creativity and openness to new vision. Once we have learned to focus, then it will require less effort and the flow will eventually become natural.

In focus, we find the vision, the inspiration, and the understanding; and in the flow, we find the expression, the experimentation, and the experience.

It is important not to overflow; otherwise we get lost in a flood of overthinking, overspeaking, and overdoing. In such a state, there is no direction to guide the expression, and things become vague and fragile. At such a point, we need to recognize that it is time for focus again.

According to necessity, a human being needs to move between focus and flow, and it is only through the *ability to discern* that we can know when and how to do this. Everything has its time. We are eternal beings working in time, so we need to know the balance between the focus of eternity—where we find truth and purpose—and the flow of time—where we find expression and experience.

Principle 4: Stepping In and Stepping Out

For any activity or relationship, to remain harmonious and successful we must know how far to step in and how far to step out. It is like a gardener, who sows seeds at the right time, steps in to plant, waters them, and then steps out of the picture to allow nature to carry on with her work. However, from time to time, he steps in again to see if there is enough water, if any insects are attacking the plants, if any food is needed. His role is to find the appropriate space for the potential beauty and uniqueness of the seeds to emerge; he does not create the flowers, but facilitates their expression.

The gardener does not step in too much; that would be called interference. After planting the seeds, he does not demand an immediate result; he does not dig them up the next day to see if they have sprouted. He plays his role and fulfills his duty, but then lets go because he understands that the blooming of the flowers is not dependent on him. Nor does he let go too much. If he did, then the plants would die from lack of care, or the insects and weeds would overpower them. He does not let go so much that he isolates himself from the process. Instead, by knowing when to step in and when to step out, he creates a respectful partnership with nature.

In the same way, we have the duty, or rather the honor, of planting positive seeds of good intention, respect, and tolerance, at the same time allowing others and the forces of the universe to be given the space to work and respond according to their time and inclination.

Very often we plant those seeds but want an immediate result: "I have shown so much patience, but he doesn't change." Or "How much longer do I have to be tolerant? I feel suppressed." We become attached to what we do, so there is no space for things to happen in their own appropriate time. Sometimes we have the wrong type of mercy, or we want to take control, thinking we know better, so we step into people's lives too much. This interference and lack of free space provokes antagonism, resentment, and conflict with others.

At other times, we get fed up with others; our tolerance and empathy is completely reduced and we say "I've had enough," or "I have to do my own thing" and so we step out, but in a selfish way: that is, we isolate ourselves from others, or from situations. We justify, or disguise, this rejection and dislike with such phrases as "I need my own space" or "Let them stand on their own feet." In actual fact, we can't be bothered any more; we have stepped too far out of the picture because we have not cultivated the patient understanding that allows the good and positive to germinate and grow in its own time.

> It is an art to know when to step back and when to step forward, but a very necessary one if well-being is to be achieved.

Principle 5: Complementarity

Harmony, well-being, and the fulfillment of individual purpose are only possible when our consciousness is inclusive, rather than exclusive: that is, a consciousness that is universal in the sense that we can recognize and appreciate the purpose and necessity of all things in life and therefore give them the space to express their innate right to be.

When people, either on an individual or collective level, become exclusive—that is, when the foundation of their identity is based on prerogative and privilege—then harmony, peace, and certainly love are lost both in the individual and in society. Individuals, societies, nations, religions, and politics become exclusive when they are attributed a particular specialty, talent, or position. While it is healthy and necessary to value *who* you are, it becomes most unhealthy and violent to become attached to your special qualities, making others feel inferior because they do not possess those same qualities. The reason for conflict, on any level, is nearly always this sense of right to dominate or suppress others, just because we feel we are better in one way or another.

Unfortunately, in modern society, both East and West, the idea of outdoing others in order to prove the value of the person or idea has taken precedence over the innate principle of life, which is complementarity.

When we learn to complement rather than compete, there
will be peace and, above all, self-respect.

Self-respect means to recognize myself as I am and thus fulfill my purpose without injury to, or comparison with, others. We all have a place within this beautiful tapestry of life; let us know it, enjoy it, express it as our right, but never overdo it because we feel our role or position is "more advanced" or "better" than others. Sometimes, when there is a sense of personal or collective inadequacy, there is the need to be recognized, which creates attachment to privilege and prerogative. When a sense of identity is based on these, it creates exclusivity.

Nature works on the principle of complementarity. This can be seen with the seasons, day and night, the continual cyclical process of birth, growth, maturity, decay, death, and rebirth. Even our bodies work on this principle. Look at the face! Each face has two eyes, one nose, one mouth, two ears, all in the right position and functioning in an appropriate way. Which of these is more important? Would you say the eyes are more important, so you would prefer to have three eyes and no nose? Or would you say the nose is more important, so you would prefer to have three noses and no ears? We cannot think like this, because it is absurd and illogical. Each feature has equal value and, when we recognize the equality of value of all things, then we stop being illogical, comparing, competing, feeling superior or inferior, or striving to be what we are not. In a society that functions, can everyone be a doctor, a builder, or a baker? Everyone has different talents and positions, because different tasks have to be fulfilled if the whole society is to run well.

> *If we examine life carefully, we realize that the recognition of this principle of complementarity is the basis of creating a peaceful and happy coexistence, because the vision and attitude of equality respects and honors the differences.*

Principle 6: The Individual and the Collective

There are two faces to the one coin: a person who wishes to live fully as a human being needs to understand that the existence of one's unique individuality has to be acknowledged, as well as the existence of the collective. One cannot exist without the other, although many people have gone to the extremes of both with very damaging results. Those systems, which develop the collective aspect at the expense of the individual, become rigid, autocratic, cruel, and uncreative, often imposing a sterile uniformity on human thought and action in the belief that this is the way to maintain harmony and order. Those systems (whether social, religious, or political) that develop individualism above everything else, create narcissism and self-indulgence, resulting in a personal sense of isolation. This alienation is often the result of not developing the values of tolerance and acceptance, which are such a necessary part of human coexistence.

Individuals who are developing spiritually feel a personal sense of value. They clearly recognize their uniqueness without any false humility and have the feeling that there is the freedom to be whatever they choose to be. Simultaneously, their sense of personal independence allows them to come close to others and work with them. They do not have selfish independence. They get close to others because they have found fulfillment in their own selves.

People who have truly discovered the value of the self will never confine themselves to, or exaggerate their worth with, an illusory identity based on labels and external achievements.

Someone who has truly found the value of the self above and beyond labels, name, fame, and approval, can effectively cooperate within the collective and interact appropriately. Such people not only feel themselves to be a part of the whole but, even more significantly, the collective feels them to be a part of the whole.

In nature, when birds have to fly to a warmer climate in winter, they flock together and start their journey as a collective. The success of the journey depends on the collective: if an individual bird does not join the group, it cannot reach the destination on its own. Birds fly in a particular formation, with an appropriate space between them as they fly. If they fly too close to each other, their wings get entangled; they lose their balance and fall. If they remain too far from each other, the formation cannot be created properly, and they are not able to ride the currents of air, which help to propel them in their flight. Furthermore, the leader of the formation does not remain the leader throughout the whole flight, but moves back and allows another to take its place. This repositioning continues throughout the flight until the destination is reached, allowing individual birds to contribute to the success of the journey.

> *The reality of life is that we are individuals within a collective whole.*

If the collective respects the space of the individual, then it functions to serve the individual's aspirations and differences. Otherwise, if the collective does not respect that space, it becomes repressive. In short, the individual needs to respect the collective and not go to the extremes of personal rights, and the collective must respect the individual and not go to the extremes in its use of systems.

Principle 7: Faith

What we believe comes true. What we believe is the reflection of our deepest-held ideas and thoughts, which, in one way or another, are present at every moment of our lives. It has been said that faith can move mountains.

The highest mountains are our negative thoughts, feelings, and ideas, which hinder our capacity to rise beyond our limits.

Faith is the energy of understanding that enables us to realize that anything is possible, even if it is not visible in front of our eyes—but, more especially, even if it is not visible in front of our reason.

The success that comes from faith is closely linked with "letting go." It is only when we let go of what we are used to, or what we have learned to depend on, that new perceptions and new possibilities are given to us.

Our life is like that of a pole vaulter. We have used many tools in our life, which at their time were valuable and necessary but now have to be discarded because other items are necessary. The same applies to people who wish for a deeper spiritual experience when they use knowledge. Knowledge is very necessary, and without it we cannot rise to the heights we wish; but, equally, at some point we have to let go of the support of knowledge and jump. To jump over the barrier of habit, custom, and comfort is not simply a matter of knowledge, but also to dare the self to enter another dimension of consciousness. To be willing to experiment requires faith and cannot be done if we remain within our comfort zones.

With faith, it is not necessary to analyze and know everything in detail before doing something.

> *All that is needed are a few basic facts, and then we can take action. When we drive a car, do we insist on knowing how the engine works in detail before driving it? Do we know the mechanical details of an elevator before we use it? Most people are only aware of the basic functions, and this is all they need to carry out the action. However, they do have the faith that the car has been correctly constructed to do its job safely, and that by pressing a few buttons the elevator will take them to wherever it is they want to go. In the modern world, there is a tendency to overthink, to want to control and direct every outcome; but such a life lacks spontaneity and simplicity.*

Although we do need a framework, a true structure, or plan, allows space for the unexpected, the unpredictable, and the great surprise. Such a space is the window through which the light of innovation can enter. When life is overplanned, we become cemented in, unable to grow, or flow, into new horizons. Faith allows us to realize that optimum results can happen without our always having to structure or plan. Such faith is the basis for new vision; it allows us to reach beyond our limits; because we believe we are more than meets the eye, such faith is the inspirational energy of every pioneer in any field.

Principle 8: Relationship with the Unconditional Source

There is one Point of Being in the universe who is not conditioned by any need, want, or desire. Since He does not want anything, everything belongs to Him, but not in the sense of owning and controlling: rather, all things naturally gravitate to the Unconditional Source simply because pure love is given freely to all who come close. They feel that He selflessly serves, sharing all that He is, all that He has. Like a radiant Magnet beyond the limits of time and matter, beyond give and take, and beyond measurement and calculation, the Source attracts all because nothing is desired and all is given.

The love of the Unconditional Source is like spiritual sunlight. Physical sunlight awakens the flower hidden in the seed, without intrusion or taking for the self; sunlight facilitates the birth and blooming of the flower. Light, whether physical or spiritual, is selfless, complete in itself: it always adds, never subtracts. What is unconditional is always cherished to the point of worship, which is probably why God and real saints are venerated in all parts of the world. Spiritual light from the Source reveals to us our forgotten realities, our hidden potential, and our original goodness. It reveals our true selves. Then, if we wish, we can nourish and develop that awareness, but only to the extent that we maintain an open channel of communication. Otherwise, the current either short-circuits, cuts, blocks, or discharges in other directions; after a while, there is a blackout! Humanity, at the moment, is in the blackout phase.

Meditation is the mental exercise to link ourselves to that Unconditional Source. As we make that link, purification takes place, liberating the mind from the limits of "I," "my," the past, resentments, and pettiness.

During meditation, the mind lets go of the threads of the limited. Like a bird, the mind flies up and connects to God. This connection is not difficult when the mind is truly in love with knowing the truth and not just trying to demand, cajole, or beg God for something for selfish reasons. When there is just a desire for connection, the soul feels a magnetic pull that enables it to fly beyond all impossible barriers such as "I can't," "How?", and "No time!". Connection fills the soul with a spiritual strength that keeps it constantly positive, uninfluenced by any external negativity.

Meditation helps us to gain this inner spiritual strength, especially when we use it in our everyday life. To maintain such strength, we require a daily connection and recharge every morning. In the same way that the body needs daily nourishment to give it the strength to work during the day, so the soul needs the sustenance of silence. In silence, the human being finds a personal and benevolent friendship with God, who is not only there to listen and to help: most of all, He is just there. Human beings have completely lost the simple enjoyment of His presence; they feel they have to ask for something, say something, or chant something. But it is enough just to be still in the silence of that spiritual meeting and be content.

12

Balance and Harmony

HARMONY WITHIN THE SELF AND WITH OTHERS is based on the accuracy of three aspects of remembrance: the ability to *disconnect, connect, and reconnect.*

> *When I disconnect my thoughts from outside influences, stepping back from actions and words, then I can go into silence and connect with the self.*

To plug into the self, I use the thought: Om Shanti. This thought is the current that activates my eternal resource of peace and the qualities that emanate from this peace. The first step in meditation is always to connect with the self: what we call the inward step.

> *The next step in meditation is vertical, where, within one second, my concentrated thought connects my mind with the Supreme Source of Peace.*

Silence and love give the mind wings to break the pull of gravity and to fly and unite with the One, who is the purest point of energy in the universe. This vertical connection from the point of the self, the soul, to the point of the universe, the Supreme Soul, gives the mind fresh new energy. This fresh energy is divine spiritual power and cannot be found in, or taken from, a human being. Therefore, if I wish to recharge myself, to rediscover and restore the original balance and harmony within myself, the second movement made by my mind must be vertical.

Today, when human beings seek love, meaning, and purpose, they first connect horizontally rather than vertically. This leads to a greater loss of energy and eventually dissatisfaction and emptiness. The vertical connection liberates the self from becoming dependent on someone else and from having too many expectations.

After the vertical connection, there can then be the horizontal connection with others, that is, with the outside or external.

The horizontal movement can be called "reconnection." When we have taken the other two steps (first inward and then upward), we reconnect with others on the basis of openness and sharing, rather than selfishness and need. At this point, there is a real relationship that is respectful and balanced, rather than a relationship of wanting, taking, or exploiting. We have come to understand that when we are well with ourselves, we will be well with others.

All three points of connection are necessary for good emotional and spiritual health.

If I am only connected inwardly, there is a great danger of arrogance and being lost in only myself. If I am only connected to the Supreme Source with little reference to myself or others, there is the danger of becoming rigid, fanatical, and unrealistic. If I am overfocused on others, then a dependency is created, which results in conflict and disappointment. The latter is an inevitable result of over-focusing on relationships with others, thinking I will receive my happiness and sense of purpose from them.

> *When I do reconnect with the outside world, it can only be done effectively from the vantage point of connection with the self and with the One.*

This three-point connection can be depicted in the form of a triangle with the self as a point, then the vertical movement upward to the Supreme Point:

Then the horizontal connection to others:

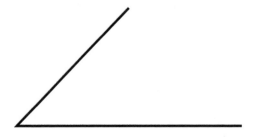

Others need to have their own independent and personal connection with the Supreme Point to revitalize and renew their own consciousness. In this way, the triangle of harmonious energy becomes complete:

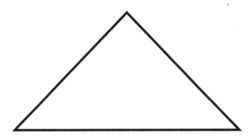

All three points need to be equidistant—not too much one way, or the other. The "equidistant triangle" in ancient mathematics was the symbol of harmony. Harmony, peace, order, and balance is what is natural in human life; if we wish to return to that condition, we need to realize the importance of equidistant relationships. It requires constant attention to keep the three in balance and in working order. Otherwise, when we get overfocused on any one of the three, we become inflexible. This inflexibility causes us to go out of balance, and the result is disharmony and disunity, which can also be called "violence," an unnatural condition—or even "hell" if it reaches an extreme point.

In order to maintain a balance between the three, I need silence: times of introspection when I can check the flow of my relationships. This checking mechanism protects, sustains, and develops the qualities of these three points.

☙ 13 ❧

Motivation

MEDITATION, IN THE FORM OF REFLECTION AND EXAMINATION, helps me to create and maintain my motivation. For newness and clarity of perception, ideals, and aims, we need to relax our grip on old habits, on old ways of thinking and seeing, and thus create a space for something new and inspirational.

> *Motivation is an inner positive energy, a combination of enthusiasm and clear perception that enables us to accomplish a task.*

Motivation keeps us determined and on course; otherwise, it is so easy to be distracted by problems, novelties, and laziness. What does motivation do? It moves us from one reality to another, from where I am to where I wish to be. Motivation is sustained when a sense of purpose, identity, and contribution is being fulfilled.

When we want to reactivate our motivation, we need to examine the following:

- What do I want?

- What do I wish for?

- What do I value?

- What do I need?

- What do I enjoy?

- What do I understand? and, especially,

- What do I love?

When we sit down and reflect on the answers to these questions, then these reflections become the basis for activating new insights and new tasks, and for reactivating those insights and tasks, which we have forgotten to pay proper attention to and, consequently, haven't developed properly. Throughout life it is necessary, from time to time, to stand back, become silent, and redefine, re-evaluate, and experiment, over and over again, with what we know, or what we think we know. It is a simple exercise which, if done sincerely, stimulates newness in our thoughts and in our motivational pattern.

Therefore, to change or widen my pattern, I need to

- redefine

- re-examine

- reorient

- relearn

Then newness, creativity, and quality are generated.

Successful motivation depends on having a clear aim. How much do I believe in my aim? Faith in my aim determines the quality of effort and the willingness to meet challenges. There will be successful renewal of motivation when I realize that there is always the opportunity to exercise the power of choice.

Another question that helps us in sustaining motivation is: "What is really most important to me: product, or process?" Process entails growth, development, and learning: a cultivation of the awareness and resources of the self and others. To be product-oriented tends to overfocus on result, without enough care or attention to the underlying processes needed to arrive at that result. The quick-fix method, the "success in 7 days" formula, does not really work, at least not permanently. If we look at nature, we see that her beauty and her strength are the combined result of time and process. For example, a huge oak tree, the roses in the garden, and the changing of the seasons do not happen instantly. There is always space and time given for particular processes to function.

For a process to happen effectively, I need to prioritize: that is, to make the best use of my time, energy, and resources.

To prioritize, I also need to recognize and refuse clever excuses (for example, "there is no time") and create a timetable that is realistic and functional. As I prioritize my values, the type of motivation I have becomes clearer. Is my motivation materialistic, or spiritual? The results of the two are very different:

Materialistic motivation is based on ambition, competition, and a desire for position. We often believe we cannot succeed without these, and so we think and act on the basis of these values. The results often include conflict, fear, attachment, jealousy, possessiveness, and overidentification of the self with a role, a position, which makes us feel threatened by anyone who is more talented or more praised. For example, when motivation is materialistic, there is always the fear of loss that, in turn, creates uneasiness, stress, and worry.

Spiritual motivation is based on enthusiasm for a task, rather than blind ambition; cooperation with the uniqueness of others, rather than being in competition with those differences. Finally, the feeling to serve through whatever talent, position, or role I have: to serve a need rather than exploit a need is quality service.

The results of spiritual motivation are respect; harmony; individual and collective well-being; a sense of purpose; and the feeling of a deep fulfilment in one's being.

Spiritual motives such as cooperation, sharing, caring, integrity, and respect create quality in the aim, the task, and the methodology used. Meditation, in the form of reflection, always helps me to re-examine and redefine my aims, my processes, and the reasons I am doing what I am doing.

∞ 14 ∞

Communication

A GREAT DEAL OF OUR COMMUNICATION IS NONVERBAL, and we rarely realize the impact that it has on others. Our tone of voice, our body language (particularly our eyes and face), our attitudes, and our feelings are constantly in communication with others, expressing anger, fear, love, trust, rejection—in short, all our emotions. We cannot hide what we mean; we may do so for a while, but the truth eventually emerges.

> *In order to communicate clearly, the primary step is silence:*
> *that is, the ability to listen.*

In addition to listening, communication is also about sharing, understanding, and enjoying what the other has to offer. Genuine communication heals and nurtures. Communication is not just with others, but also with the self, with God, and even with nature. Being still, focused, and open enables us to tune in to others so that we can respond in an appropriate and meaningful way, not simply in a mechanical way.

What are the blocks to positive communication? When I communicate, do I reflect, or deflect what I mean? Is what I am communicating clear, or confused to others?

Here are some common reasons for blocks to communication:

- A plethora of thoughts, words, and actions sends us into overload. As a result, we are unable to think clearly because we lose the essence of what is trying to be conveyed through a jumble and jungle of thoughts and words.

- Being too lost in our own emotions or ideas. When this happens, we do not listen attentively to others.

- Remembering the past in a negative way. This does not allow me to tune in properly to my present and my future. When I cannot communicate properly with the needs of the present time, then I lose current opportunities.

- Lack of sincerity. When my thoughts and feelings are honest and respectful, then the hearts of others will open to me. A positive highway of trust will be built to enable communication to flow positively.

- Negative perceptions and feelings about others, how I visualize someone or how I label them. Negative feelings, no matter how well hidden, are always eventually communicated to others on a subtle, nonverbal level. When this silent language is spoken and caught, it creates an atmosphere of tension and uneasiness.

- Not letting go of negative perceptions and feelings. This creates tension in communication. The only method to renew my relationship with others is to let go of negativity on a daily basis, to prevent it from building up. Far too often, the buildup happens without us even noticing it and, in one moment, we wonder why positive feedback is not forthcoming.

- Lack of silence. To go deep into myself and put my thoughts and feelings into the quarantine of silence enables them to become positive. The quarantine of silent relaxation defuses anger and the blame and complaints that often go with it.

What are the ways to improve communication?

- Listen with *both* ears. I should be an active listener by tuning in fully and being fully present with the person and with the moment. If I am not, I listen through one ear and let it out of the other, or I only half listen, which inevitably creates misunderstandings.

- Understand where the other person is coming from. Do not just assume, imagine, or judge; when we do this, our critical vision inhibits others from expressing what they wish to say. Then, because of wrong or half-right assumptions, others are not given the possibility to move, or express, outside my imposed frame of reference. To give others a true chance to express themselves, I must not place my own frames around them.

- Think before speaking. This is not something new; but however often we hear it, we forget to apply it. To think before speaking means to show consideration to the other, and then we say the right thing, at the right time, in the right way.

- Say what you mean, always. When you speak with courage and a calm self-confidence without force, then communication is honest, open, clear, and trusted. Courage doesn't mean to say what you think others want to hear. If you lack courage because of the need for approval and acceptance, or because of a lack of confidence, then communication and the consequent relationship remain superficial and artificial. No one feels satisfied with this situation.

- Learn the language of silence. It is the basis of right intention, positive feelings, and clear attitudes. In this language, there is only one grammar: honesty and kindness. Honesty creates clarity, and kindness creates respectfulness.

When we take time to reflect on our level of communication with everyone we meet, the realizations we have in silence will be manifested in the higher quality and ease of interaction that we will find in all relations, be it with the self, with others, or with the Supreme Source of Light.

∞ 15 ∞

Overcoming Fear

FEAR COMES DAILY AND OFTEN INTO OUR LIVES, in the forms of stress, worry, anxiety, and a variety of other wasteful and negative things. For example, stress is one of the biggest diseases of the twenty-first century. Originally the word "stress" was only used for the pressure, or tension, exerted on a machine: engineers build in a calculation for stress to ensure that the machine functions correctly. Gradually the term has become more and more popularly used to describe the state of human beings.

When we try to describe stress, a whole chain of words such as "push," "pull," "pressure," "more," or "deadlines" come to mind. To have to produce, to do more and more and to be better and better at it, creates a lot of tension, which comes from the fear of not being able to achieve the result on time. The materialistic values of getting, having, accumulating, and outdoing others in the form of ambition, competition, and position produce a lot of stress.

When we are stressed, we are certainly overloaded. We think and speak too much, and we overreact, all of which affect both body and mind negatively. The worst thing is that this becomes a habit, which is often uncontrolled; so the simple remedy of stopping and relaxing is not considered as a remedy. Some even regard it as a useless waste of time.

However, before we explore how to overcome fears generally, let us look at some of the types of fear human beings suffer from:

- The unknown — for example, death or a new situation.

- Loneliness — sometimes people fear loneliness to the extent that they cannot bear their own company, preferring to lose themselves in superficial relationships and activities.

- The future — as the crises of the world increase, whether political, economic, environmental or social, this creates, or adds to, personal and collective fear of the future.

- Illness — sometimes, because of fear of disease, people make their sickness worse than it is, or live in dread of getting something horrible.

- Other people — usually this is the greatest fear of all: fear of others' anger, rejection, judgment, and violence.

- Failure — some people avoid doing something, or choose not to act, because their fear of failure paralyzes initiative and confidence.

- Authority — this can be fear of a parent, of a director, even of God. Because authority has often been misused or misrepresented in order to control and suppress people, it is a normal consequence that fear, in the form of suspicion and mistrust, has become such a negative force, both personally and collectively, in society.

There are many reasons for these types of fear, but the main ones include:

- Past experiences, which brought disappointment, insecurity, closure, or wariness.

- Lack of faith in one's self and in others.

- Needing to be approved, to belong, or to be accepted, which can create stressful behavior strategies aimed at achieving these things.

- The habit of seeing things negatively.

One of the greatest products of fear is doubt.

When a person is lost in doubt, he or she cannot believe in the solutions and answers given, not even to the point of experimenting with them, trying to see if they could work. Doubt in an extreme form creates such uncertainty and insecurity that a person suffers from mental, and even emotional, paralysis. There is either a freeze-up, or a panic, where no initiative for being positive is possible. The mind is plagued by questions of "How?" "When?" "Why?" or "What?" Questions are not posed to really find answers, but to prolong hesitation or keep the self on the defensive or in a state of non-commitment, not really listening or wanting to know. To inquire is a different thing from doubt; when there is inquiry, there are constructive questions, an openness to learn, and a willingness to experiment.

When there is any type of fear, which may be expressed through doubt, jealousy, secrecy, or competitiveness, there is neither openness nor willingness. At the core of it all, there is the fear of loss, either of a person, a position, a possession, or one's image. All fears, whether subtle or gross, result in dependence, expectation, and, ultimately, conflict, either with one's own self or with others.

How Can We Overcome Fear?

Before participating or reacting, we often need to relax, become calm, and observe so that our contribution is appropriate and positive.

Learn to observe:

How do I see myself?

- As valuable?
- With the right to be?
- As someone I can face?
- As someone I like, accept, and respect?

How do I see others?

- Friends?
- Enemies?
- Teachers?
- Supports?
- Extensions to me?
- Valuable?

How do I see life? Primarily as:

- Joy or pain?
- Gift or curse?
- Game or battle?
- Learning or losing?

If I go through these questions quietly and slowly and give myself time to think about them, the answers will make me aware of whether I am building walls or bridges in my life. Are there only bridges, or only walls, or both? More bridges, or more walls? The negative answer is a wall; the positive answer is a bridge.

Here are some ways to build more bridges and fewer walls:

Trust

Learn to trust, because trusting the self, others, and life opens unforeseen possibilities. Do not worry too much about "if I am cheated," "if the other is not true," if, if, if—leave the "ifs," and just do. As is said, "nothing ventured, nothing gained."

Faith

Jump over barriers; do not make them into excuses. If we do not accept challenges, our life is one of a "boring safety" whose foundation is fear of newness, fear of change. It may appear safe and comfortable, but it is an illusory security that can break at any time, in any way.

Acceptance

Mistakes, setbacks, failures, disappointments are part of the growing and knowing process and should not be condemned or feared. Every human being has gone through it, is going through it, and will continue to do so.

Remaining Light

All things have their meaning and—if not now, eventually—I will understand that meaning. It is healthy for mind and body not to carry the burden of exaggeration and lack of perspective.

Life Is a Game

Know the rules and play it well. A good player is aware, then easy, tolerant, and flexible, does not get stuck on a scene, a rule, or any other player for too long, gives due respect and attention but keeps moving. A good player plays his own part and does not try to play the part of others.

Self-respect

Let me acknowledge my spiritual reality as a human being with quality resources inside that need to always be opened up and used. I do not need to accept false support from the outside, such as name, fame, and praise. I am what I am because of what is inside me. My reference point is that which is eternal and valuable inside; then there cannot be the fear of being damaged.

Silence and Positive Outlook

When we realize the importance of being silent and still from time to time, then our positivity toward self and life is re-examined and renewed. Otherwise, the speed and immensity of negative forces, whether from our selves or from others, will certainly make us fearful.

Let me remove myself from the pressures of life and learn to break the chains of fear that bind me and prevent me from making spiritual progress.

∽ 16 ∽

Next Steps

THE MIND NEEDS TO RELAX, TO REFRESH ITSELF, if a person is to feel positive and strong to live each day peacefully and efficiently. When this is recognized, time for silence every day is prioritized.

Creating a space for silence within is important, but simultaneously creating such a place on a physical level is also necessary. Where I live, I can create a corner or a room, which is used only for this purpose, to relax and concentrate on inner peace. In that space, there is the opportunity each morning to prepare for the coming day and, in the evening, to unburden the mind of wasteful thoughts and feelings that have accumulated.

One aspect, which enables us to achieve success in meditation—or in anything, for that matter—is the attention to being systematic in our practice. Being systematic—that is, the daily practice of morning preparation and evening clearing—will keep the mind healthy. A healthy mind is light and focused, not distracted or burdened easily.

Naturally, having the inner discipline to practice meditation by one's self is necessary because, in reality, only I can step into my mind and bring it long-term benefit. However, the spiritual company of others who share the same aim and practice can also be of great value. To practice meditation collectively, to discuss and listen to others' processes and methods, gives us perspective. We learn from others as well as from ourselves.

How do we practically begin to create and sustain this path of meditation?

1. Attend a Meditation Center

The beginning point is knowledge, or understanding. It is not possible to begin this journey without some kind of map. There are centers of Raja Yoga, which provide these maps to help a person begin his or her practice of meditation. Information is shared about how the mind functions and about the power of positivity, spiritual values, and the art of effective concentration. All these maps help us to know ourselves better and, when translated into our personal daily lives, give us strength in the form of self-respect and happiness.

A Raja Yoga meditation center is a spiritual school where we can learn the original basics of true living; it is a spiritual clinic where we receive the understanding of how to apply the healing medicines of peace, trust, and respect in our relationships; and it is a spiritual family where we realize that each one has a uniqueness and goodness that needs to be appreciated and genuinely accepted, and where we pay attention to avoiding the trap of focusing on weaknesses and the role of others.

The key to all this is to remember.

To remember that each day is a chance to learn, to heal, and to see the inherent goodness of others. When we forget these things, we become polluted by stress and animosity. How to remember when there is so much to get done, so much negativity to face? The theory is inspiring; but in practice, how can it all be achieved?

2. Use "Traffic Control"

Besides going to the center, there is one system, developed in Raja Yoga, called "traffic control." As mentioned previously, this is a method to check and control the flow and type of thoughts that we create. Are the thoughts wasteful, useful, necessary, positive, or peaceful? About six times a day, we stop, step inside, put on the brake of remaining in the thought "I am a peaceful being," cool ourselves, and, while watching and discerning the actions and feelings of others, we understand when and how to re-enter the flow of interaction with them. This practice is done for only about three minutes; but, if done regularly, it has a very positive impact on our daily lives.

> *To remember my original peaceful state during certain moments of the day creates a space for me to recharge and to be released from accumulated negativities which have influenced my mind without my realizing it.*

3. Meditate with Others

Another great help in maintaining a stable grounding on the path of meditation is collective practice. Through personal practice, I keep my sense of responsibility intact and remain independent. However, without losing these, I can also integrate with others, valuing and learning from their experiences and perceptions: the group dynamic brings us to another level of experience, a space of mutual experience and learning. We learn from everyone, everywhere, all the time; it depends on our willingness to accept certain realities. For example, our attitude toward time is more responsible and positive when we are more reflective about how we live.

We often live too much in the past, or in the future, and so do not realize that the present is the bridge to changing the negativity of the past and to creating a confident future. We do not cross this bridge because we live by—or are too influenced by—the other two time zones.

> *Remember that NOW is the opportunity where newness on any level can be created.*

In the depths of meditation, we not only understand, but experience—as a primary truth—that the wounds, disappointments, and anger of the past are healed and that our ideals, hopes, and aims for the future can be made real. Meditation, especially, develops an open-hearted learning attitude; it develops the ability to step back and observe, which is of utmost necessity to break free from the judgments, opinions, and criticisms that consistently clog and cloud perception, and consequently the quality of our life. As the mind opens, it becomes more neutral, no longer invaded by fears, labels, and dependencies. It throws them all away. The mind moves into another gear—freedom.

For this to happen, as already mentioned, I need to start each day with positive silence. Before work, before breakfast, before doing anything, let me step inside myself for a little while. In this space of introspection, I connect with my original spiritual qualities; I discard the stale things from yesterday, if some are still remaining, and begin today fresh. Having connected with the best in myself, it helps me to live more consciously so that I am able to deal with everything more effectively.

> *The main point of any journey is to start.*

Sometimes we hesitate, sometimes we make excuses, but we must not give in to these. When we accept the challenge to try, the journey begins.

When we agree to take the first steps, success is there waiting for us. Faith in ourselves brings optimism to what we do. Optimism and faith open the Horizon of Possibility, an inner knowing of what good could be there which, as yet, I cannot see or even imagine.

It is said: "Nothing ventured, nothing gained." So why not venture? Why not gain?

About the Brahma Kumaris World Spiritual University

http://www.bkwsu.org

International Headquarters

P.O. Box No. 2, Mount Abu 307501
Rajasthan, India
Tel: (+91) 2974-38261 through 38268
Fax: (+91) 2974-38952
Email: abu@bkindia.com

International Coordinating Office & Regional Office for Europe and the Middle East

Global Co-operation House
65-69 Pound Lane
London NW10 NHH, UK
Tel: (+44) 208 727 3350
Fax: (+44) 208 727 3351
Email: london@bkwsu.org

Regional Offices

Africa

Global Museum for a Better World
Maua Close, off Parklands Road, Westlands
P.O. Box 123, Sarit Center
Nairobi, Kenya
Tel: (+254) 20-374 3572
Fax: (+254) 20-374 2885
Email: nairobi@bkwsu.org

Australia and Southeast Asia

78 Alt Street
Sydney, NSW 2131, Australia
Tel: (+61) 2 9716 7066
Fax: (+61) 2 9716 7795
Email: ashfield@au.bkwsu.org

The Americas and the Caribbean

Global Harmony House
46 S. Middle Neck Rd.
Great Neck, NY 11021, USA
Tel: (+1) 516 773 0971
Fax: (+1) 516 773 0976
Email: newyork@bkwsu.org

Russia, CIS, and the Baltic Countries

2 Gospitalnaya Ploschad, Build. 1
Moscow – 111020, Russia
Tel: (+7) 499-263 02 47
Fax: (+7) 499-261 32 24
Email: Moscow@bkwsu.org

Brahma Kumaris Publications
http://www.bkpublications.com
enquiries@bkpublications.com

Index